The Trail That Leads to You

Published by Transformational Press Company
Copyright © 2024 Heidi Fischer

All rights reserved. No part of the contents of this book may be reproduced by any means without the written permission of the publisher.

Medical disclaimer: Although the publisher and the author have made every effort to ensure that the information in this book was correct at press time and while this publication is designed to provide accurate information in regard to the subject matter covered, the publisher and the author assume no responsibility for errors, inaccuracies, omissions, or any other inconsistencies herein and hereby disclaim any liability to any party for any loss, damage, or disruption caused by errors or omissions, whether such errors or omissions result from negligence, accident, or any other cause. This publication is meant as a source of valuable information for the reader, however it is not meant as a substitute for direct expert assistance. If such level of assistance is required, the services of a competent professional should be sought.

Publishing and design services: MelindaMartin.me
Editor: Gail Fallen
ISBN: 979-8-218-37579-9

The Trail That Leads to You

A Journey toward Self-Love, Transformation, and Inner Peace

Heidi Fischer

To my husband:
Thank you for making our dreams a reality.

And to my babies:
May you never lose courage
to follow your inner compass.

CONTENTS

Part 5

Part 6

Part 7

INTRODUCTION

I used to think life would provide me a black-and-white narrative. That in my life I would be presented simple choices where I could easily determine right versus wrong and good versus bad. That things would progress in a linear fashion and always be straightforward, to the point, and exactly as they appeared or seemed. My black-and-white mentality kept me thinking that my course would be easily identifiable and clear.

I believed that when someone said something, it was true; that you kept your same close-knit friends until your hair turned white, and you would live in your same town—maybe even the same house—for the entirety of your life. Although life changes, and things may shift, they would do so in orderly fashion and an expected timeline: fall in love, go to college, get married, start a family, and live happily ever after. There wouldn't be a lot of surprises or twists and turns because life is predictable.

As I grew up, my life was carefree and easy in my small town. It felt as though my path was laid out in front of me and sharply defined with little wiggle room for venturing off course. And besides, wouldn't it be wild and irresponsible to think it could be lived in any other manner than the cookie-cutter blueprint I assumed as a young child? Yet soon the repercussions of my choices shook things up and brought on an overwhelming feeling of being torn and questioning where I belonged. What once felt black and white became a never-ending gray area which altered what I thought would have been my sure and steady course.

Feeling torn escalated into my new daily emotion. While it had a tight hold on my heart, it left no trace for someone to notice on the exterior. It consumed my mind once I lived two separate lives in two independent places for years. It was the perfect adjective to describe my heart as I would say "See you later" to my first true love, then resume my daily life without him. It was the gnawing feeling that lingered inside, but I would choose to play it safe instead of following my inner compass.

The torn feeling stuck to me like a barnacle to its host, and I often questioned my predicament: where I was meant to be and what I should be doing with my life. My path steered me toward multiple forks in the road where my precariousness would take over; I would waver in my decision of which route I should choose every single time.

But isn't this how most amazing stories start? A captivating narrative often begins with setting the scene in an engaging place and time before the inevitable friction that has been brewing within the protagonist is exposed. Plagued with uncertainty, the main character feels ambivalent between a call to action or to instead stay on their safe and set course. It's likely the character bases their decision of what to do on the opinions of others or weighs in the comfortable life they would be forgoing. They may solely consider what they would be giving up instead of all they could gain.

As the main character in my own story, I allowed the fear of failure, societal pressures, and lack of self-esteem to impede my effort to truly live life. My mind was my biggest enemy, my body deeply felt the emotions of my day to day, and my soul was discouraged.

In my efforts to tightly control my life experience, I was missing the beauty and importance of the duality of life. I viewed life's hurdles as hindrances and the detours as devastating endings to how I envisioned my world should turn. My energy was placed on resisting sadness or negativity and instead embracing fun and life's pleasures to substantiate the impression that my life was top notch—just like those impeccable Instagram accounts you follow. This created unsettling feelings and fostered perpetual disappointment within me, while my alternative option would have been to adjust my attitude or goals. I didn't consider that even the tiniest of decisions—like changing my mind—had the ability to create a massive shift or entirely different result for me.

The Butterfly Effect is a theory used in scientific circles to explain how small changes can create significant differences to an otherwise predictable outcome.[1] Little did I know, tiny steps in the right direction were only part of my missing piece. My future wasn't just being decided by a destiny or definition, but also by my chosen mindset and perspective.

In my story, there were small flickers: conversations exchanged, sermons heard, phrases on billboards, and the right timing that all contributed to create the change I so desperately needed within. All of these instances compounded with key characters generated a larger-than-life outcome. They were my continuous glimmers of hope in the midst of dark shadows.

I hope my story serves as a catalyst to perseverance . . . that as long as you have a pulse, you can change your mindset, which can inevitably change your life. I hope you feel empowered to dig deeper into the purpose of your own story to allow freedom within. I hope you notice your leading lights, understand your trail traveled, embrace your shadow, and make meaning from any brokenness or unacknowledged sadness covered up deep inside to allow you to fully live your story.

Part 1

Do not go where the path may lead,
go instead where there is no path and leave a trail.

—Ralph Waldo Emerson

1

Perspective

It was 4:00 a.m. When the morning snuck up on my weary body, I realized how awful this early in the morning felt. My oldest sister delicately touched my shoulder and told me it was time to get dressed to catch our bus. I took a deep breath and sat up on the edge of my rock-hard bed in the shared space with my sisters and other strangers. The hall light was peacefully welcoming adventure into my room that early hour. I could see my clothes laid out for the day: yoga pants, a purple University of Washington shirt, my North Face fleece, socks, and tennis shoes.

My sisters were awake and waiting for me to catch our bus. I wasn't worried since I consider myself to be fairly low maintenance when it comes to getting ready. In minutes, I got dressed; brushed my teeth; threw my hair in a high, messy bun; grabbed my purse and camera; and we were out the door. I left my phone shoved inside my backpack, which was also crammed full of clothes for our three-week trip. My phone was turned off for the duration of our time in South America since I didn't opt for international service while abroad and needed the space that being disconnected provided.

As we stepped outside our hostel, it was pitch black, with just a few city lights bordering the main road as we headed toward the buses. Once we approached them, we saw crowds of people shivering in their jackets, huddling together to stay warm. We were fortunate to be a brisk walk away from the pickup location, but that's all due to my oldest sister's planning. Whenever we took vacations, she was the mastermind behind the itinerary, and she always did a spectacular job. I was fortunate to reap the benefits of her skills by taking big trips to beautiful locations on small budgets.

We waited with the other tourists, then started loading onto the buses. I sat down on the freezing charter seat, and shortly after, we were on our way, embarking on an incredible journey while the rest of the world was still asleep. Within the first ten minutes of our drive, we could feel the elevation change as our driver steered up the winding roads and we started ascending the mountains. Once we arrived at our drop-off location, we filed off the bus and crowded around the large information signs. Our guide said, "All right everyone, there's a heavy fog this morning. Be mindful of where you step, as there are uneven surfaces and animals in the vicinity. We will explore the grounds this morning, eat lunch, and head back later today."

My sisters and I exchanged glances. *Animals?*

The fog was so thick, we could feel its density. When I extended my hand in front of my face, my palm was hazy. This wasn't the view we anticipated having from our early morning start of touring Machu Picchu. With not much to do or see in the fog, we learned from other tourists there was an optional hike. Since we had time to kill, we headed in that direction.

What started out as a flat surface quickly transitioned into steep steps circling around and around. We weren't missing out on anything down below in the fog, so we took our time on our climb.

Once we got to what felt like the top, we walked over to where others were seated. From this vantage point, there was nothing above us or below us. We were at such a high elevation that clouds were all our eyes could see. Yet after about a half hour passed, a clearing opened where we had visibility of the lush green landscape beneath us. As the clouds shifted, I could not believe what I saw; it was then I understood exactly what we had climbed.

We hiked Huayna Picchu, the tallest peak of Machu Picchu, known as the "Incan Citadel." We were sitting almost nine thousand feet above sea level with a view of the archaeological site down below. Not only were the impressive ruins covering a large section of the mountainside in the Andes range, but they were also amid massive green mountains that seemingly emitted a magical aura. This landmark, established around 1450 AD, is believed to have been constructed for the emperor at that time. Some theorized it was a religious site the Incas built as it was perfectly positioned among the sun, moon, stars, mountains, trees, water, rocks, wind, and heavens.[1]

It was a surreal moment for me. Often when I would visit landmarks of importance, it felt like a checkmark on a hypothetical bucket list. When I studied abroad, I saw the Eiffel Tower in Paris and the Colosseum in Rome, and they both felt exactly the same: "Been there, done that." But at this moment, at the top of one of the Seven Wonders of the World, I had never felt so in awe of a historic structure. I couldn't help but think how spiritually inept I felt inside because I couldn't take it all in. I felt smitten. I felt connected. I felt as though I was exactly where I was meant to be.

For the past five years, this was what I had been searching for: a sign or confirmation that I was in the right place and headed down the right path. Prior to that moment, I felt as though I was on an endless quest for my purpose. At the age of twenty-two, I was merely six months into my first job out of college, which gave me no feelings of fulfillment and instead only intensified my stress. Yet I chose to put my head down, do the work, and continue trudging forward in a career I hated but checked the boxes in life of things society tells you to do to achieve happiness.

I felt a constant tug on my soul in the midst of my pursuit, paired with the voice inside my head questioning if I was actually doing what I should be in life. I was constantly looking for answers.

Maybe I needed to practice more yoga and that would achieve inner peace to counter the endless uncertainty I felt, I thought.

However, being here and experiencing Machu Picchu, I received my sign. I had an answer. Deep in my heart I knew I was about to change course and head toward the right path. I knew I was destined for something more than settling down at a young age, getting married, having babies, and staying in my hometown.

At the top of Huayna Picchu, while I had questioned so much in my life up until that moment, I finally, *finally* had an overwhelming feeling that no matter what road I had taken to get here, *this was exactly where I was meant to be*. There were still a lot of unknowns in my life: I didn't know my next step with my soul-sucking career, I impatiently awaited details of my friend's hospitalization after his life-threatening accident that occurred just three days before my departure for Peru, and I still wanted the stars to align for me to be reunited with my first true love. So, while the familiarity of feeling torn lingered, which for years was a constant tug that I needed to be in two places at once, this stop was a requisite for my well-being. I needed this confirmation. I needed this clarity.

We made our way back down to the base of the Huayna Picchu trail. And those animals the guide had previously mentioned? They were chill and friendly llamas that roamed the ruins. The sky was now completely clear, allowing for an unobstructed view of Machu Picchu amidst the mountainside. It was vast, green, and picture perfect. There were other tourists exploring the grounds, and I loved seeing the sparkle in their eyes as if to confirm they felt as in awe of it all as I did.

These structures, built thousands of years ago in a steep ravine on the tops of the tallest mountains, were here. They were here all along. We just needed to find them in the clouds. Even though we had no visibility for hours, we didn't let it ruin our day. We climbed a citadel, waited it out, and eventually witnessed with our own eyes the beauty of Machu Picchu that had been hiding in the fog.

Sometimes, things may not be readily apparent to us or in our current view. It may require time, space, or traveling an unexpected trail to gain a different perspective or outlook in our day or in our lives. There are times when obstacles need to be navigated, clouds need to shift, or you simply need to change your mindset and patiently wait for the unimaginable to appear.

So how did I get to this point in my life? Let me do my best to make a long story short.

2

Home

When observing my hometown of Lynden, Washington, an outsider may appreciate its quaint appearance and flawless manicured lawns. With a windmill on Front Street, the Dutch influence is obvious to the naked eye, but it's also felt in your soul. There's a phrase that says, "A Dutch person will ask you how your day is, and then actually *listen* to what you say thereafter."

Lynden had its name on the map due to its substantial harvest of raspberries and the large number of dairy farms. If you live in Lynden, you can't drive from one side of town to the other without seeing someone you know paired with a friendly smile and wave. The population at the time I called it home was around ten thousand people.

I would describe our quaint town as a utopia. At least that's how it felt to me as a young child growing up. As far as I knew, not a lot of bad things went on, and if they did, they were never talked about. I had the preconceived notion that everyone was happy all the time. It appeared as though everyone went to church, they were thankful for what they had, and they all had enough. I was often reminded of this in our kitchen, complete with outdated wallpaper and a frame in the shape of a loaf of bread that read, *Give thanks with a grateful heart.*

Since I grew up this way—a simple life, with little exposure to the outside world—being thankful came easy for me. I didn't realize until I was much older how fortunate I was to have the childhood I did. My mom had the rule of "No TV before 10 a.m." She was smart because by the time 10 a.m. rolled around, my sisters and I were already off playing in the Fishtrap Creek, which ran through our backyard, or exploring the other side of the water full of bushes and trees that we called "trails" and would completely forget about the television.

Summer nights were spent riding bikes to Aries Market to purchase multiple Laffy Taffys at five cents apiece or rallying the neighborhood kids to play Kick the Can until dusk. We would play for hours since the sun would set at 9 o'clock at that time of year. If it was raining, my oldest sister, also known as our ringleader, would craft games or performances for us to join in. We would sing and create choreographed dances to songs like "Barbara Ann" by the Beach Boys, "So Long, Farewell" from *The Sound of Music*, or the "Macarena." I often insisted on participating dressed up in a tutu. This likely prompted our parents to establish a rule that there was no singing at the dinner table. It was probably one of their only moments of peace and quiet throughout the day.

Our 4,200-square-foot home included a large unfinished daylight basement where there was enough room to roller skate, or, in the summertime, we would hang a thick rope from wall to wall and drape a massive tarp we used as a fort, complete with a secret passageway for entry. There was never a shortage of activities and fun, even if we did live in the rainy Pacific Northwest corner of the United States.

My parents were Christian and simple people. Both my sisters and I attended private school since kindergarten as this was important to my parents for our upbringing. They were stable and supportive but also strict. My parents made us pay for our gas the moment we got our license as well as our cell phones, which back then was the brand-new Nokia phone that every kid in school seemed to own and play their fair share of Snake on.

Similar to most kids in my small town, I started working on the raspberry harvester at the age of fifteen with my friend Erika. On the harvester, you have one or two sorters picking out the bad or not-quite-ripe berries off the belt, while another person, the stacker, maneuvered a tray at the base of the belt to catch the fruit and would stack the flats full of raspberries. The picker would drive up and down the endless rows of berry bushes. It was a mindless job, so we would listen to mixes on our portable CD players of the latest tunes. Erika and I would attempt to sync our players, which each contained the exact same burned CD, then dance and sing to the same song while working. Having a job with your friend had a way of making it not feel like work, and our bonus was getting a tan in the summertime paired with eating the fresh raspberries.

Back when we were younger, Erika and I looked like twins. We were both blonde and athletically built, but her hair always seemed to fall perfectly into place, like a Jennifer Aniston kind of vibe, while mine would turn into a curly rat nest by the end of each day. A lot of the boys from school had crushes on Erika.

She was hilarious when she talked and always told the best stories, but she also had a way of connecting to a person on an individual level. I envied how she would let what people say roll off her back. I was always sensitive to people's opinions and had a hard time letting things go. She had no fear of speaking her mind.

One summer, to celebrate the end of berry season, our bosses took us to the waterslides. After being at the waterpark for an hour or so, Erika and I enjoyed every slide in the vicinity, then questioned what we were going to do for the rest of the day. The topic arose that "Wouldn't it be funny to go down the black hole slide and come out the other end wearing a different bathing suit?" Why this came to mind, I have no idea.

Erika and I would come up with "bright" ideas on a whim. Then, we'd exchange unspoken confirmation to partake in adventure. We made our way to the slide known as the "black hole" to do a test run. We rode down in the windy darkness together in a double inner tube. Once we got to the bottom, we agreed there was no possible way we could swap our swimsuits in such a short amount of time. Bummed, as we thought it was a brilliant plan in the making, we decided to switch just our tops.

So we attempted our plan of action. We started down the slide, and I took my top off. Knowing it would be so cliché to drop it, I held onto it with a clenched fist, waiting for Erika to swap hers out.

"It's stuck!" she said.

Surprised at her words and topless, I attempted to hold onto the sides of the slide while dragging my booty on the bottom of the slide to slow us down.

"Got it!" she said.

We traded tops and were attempting to put them on in the darkness of the slide. Quickly approaching the bottom I said, "Erika!"

"What?" she asked.

"I see the *liigghhtt*!!!"

We had arrived at the large swimming pool at the bottom of the slide. I maneuvered off the double tube into the pool to make sure my suit was tied and everything was in its place. We *did* it!

When Erika popped out of the water, she had successfully put on my top, inside out. We both started laughing. I proudly thought we should just keep our mismatched suits on the remainder of the day at the park, but she insisted we switch our tops back. So we walked over to the women's locker room to make the exchange.

While in the dressing room, she said, "Heidi!"

"What?" I asked.

"Uhh, there's a hole in your suit bottom!" she said.

Sure enough, when I had dragged my booty to slow down our ride, it created a good-sized hole in the bottom of my swimsuit.

Our shenanigans continued. Later that summer, Erika and I decided to go on a bike ride and visit our crushes, who both lived out of town. Lynden, being only seven square miles, made it so that a joyride out to the country was not that far away. Yet, being that bikes were our mode of transportation since neither of us had a driver's license, it took us an entire day to pedal out to see our boyfriends, say hi, and pedal back home. Blinded by youthful love, we never got around to telling our parents where we were going before our departure. When we arrived home from our day-long escapade, we were grounded. Erika was grounded for two days while I was grounded for a week.

My parents had a way of always making my punishments harsher. It was unfortunate that our bike ride occurred the week before our town hosted the Pacific Northwest Washington Fair, the biggest event of the summer. My boyfriend, who lived out in the country that we just took a day trip to pedal as fast as we could to say hi, would be there at the cow barn showing his calves, and I was bummed to be unable to go watch him. My parents ended up bending their grounding restrictions at the end of the week and allowed me to go see him for a day.

I had only two real boyfriends in high school by the time I was a sophomore. Both were innocent relationships that started with the question, "Will you go out with me?" Once the cow-barn boy and I broke up, I dated a guy from the public school, and my friend Lauren dated his best friend at the same time. Shortly after we were official, my parents set up rules that kept us from seeing each other outside of school events, and that is likely why our relationship fizzled out. I later learned my parents felt I was going places and didn't want a boy to be the reason I stayed in our small town instead of spreading my wings.

Erika, Lauren, and I were a part of a close group of girlfriends who were super connected day in and day out. We called ourselves the Tinky Winkies and formed the niche of six during the sixth grade. I wish I could change the name to be used in this book, but no other title does justice to a code name you thought was cool when you were twelve years old. Weekly at school, we would pass notes to each other discussing who we were crushing on, whose house we were spending the night at each Friday, and, most importantly, who was making the puppy chow and bringing the brownie mix to be consumed. We weren't mean girls, but looking back, we might have been a bit exclusive.

Lauren, who stood at 5'3", quickly became another close friend of mine when we were in the same class in fifth grade. Shortly after we became friends, I learned from my parents that Lauren and I were related: our great-grandmas were sisters, making us fourth cousins. While I played a lot of sports, she was in 4H, competing in horse competitions. We had different hobbies, but we always made time for each other. I can recall very little of my life that she wasn't a part of. I loved spending the night at her house, where we would feed her goats, ride her horses, or, in the wintertime, her dad would pull us on a kneeboard behind his snowmobile. When she would take family vacations, I was always the lucky friend chosen to join in on the occasion.

I had a fair amount of guy friends, too, but was the closest with a boy named Lucas. He was in the grade below me, and although our friend circles didn't coincide, the two of us were tight. He once told me, "Heidi, pretty sure someday I'm going to be your bridesmaid."

That's exactly how he felt for many years: he was my best guy friend. One of my earliest memories of him was the two of us chatting in the high school lobby amid his group of friends. He was on the taller side, skinny, had shaggy brown hair, and bright blue eyes. He was animated with his stories, always goofy, embodied endless energy, and we just clicked. After our first meeting, he continued to make a special effort to be my friend, seek me out at school, and catch up on my life. Back then, making friends wasn't hard, but connecting with someone effortlessly is something today I assess as pure magic.

Relationship Status: It's Complicated

It all started when I saw Zach at the public school gymnasium for a basketball tournament called the Christmas Classic, which that year commenced the day after Christmas. He was a freshman on the varsity team at the public school, and I was a junior at the private school, also on the varsity team. He was tall, cute, and confident, and I had no qualms about swooping in on a younger guy. I learned he had a girlfriend, but I had a feeling since most high school relationships aren't forever, similar to my cow-barn boyfriend or the other public-school cutie, maybe he would eventually give me a chance. I was totally into him, and he was curious to learn who I was.

During our short encounter, we had chemistry. A few months later, I was stoked to learn he was single, and that's when we started to talk. I was sixteen and he was fifteen.

The summer going into my senior year, I was co-captain of our volleyball team, and we won multiple tournaments with our unbeatable lineup. We would be returning four starters in the fall and were anticipated to be one of the top, if not *the* top team, in the state. Upon arriving home from our biggest tournament in Florida, Zach and I spent every free moment together; between me working in the berries, him working at the golf shop at

Homestead, or attending sports camps, our small windows of time spent together were cherished.

One afternoon that summer, Zach and I were sitting on the floor at my house watching TV. It was my seventeenth birthday. Zach shifted his body to face me and asked, "Will you be my girlfriend?" with a twinkle in his eye.

"Of course!" I responded, grinning ear to ear.

He initiated the inside joke that his nickname was "Zach, who started it all." Once we were dating and our friend groups started meshing, three of the other Tinky Winkies also had their eyes on younger guys at the public school. Even after some heckling of pursuing a younger boy from just about everybody, I guess you could say my relationship with Zach served as a gateway to their relationships. You can imagine it ruffled some feathers when four senior girls were interested in, and some dating, younger guys.

That summer, Zach and I had a full day off together, so we and a few of our friends went cliff jumping at Whatcom Falls. With a swimming hole at the base of the cliff and waterfalls spewing out thirty feet above, we were jumping and splashing in the water to cool us down. The state park was green, the water was refreshing, glittering in the sunshine, and it made for an exceptional afternoon, one that could be lived over and over again. Other long summer evenings were spent together playing late-night tennis matches or creating countless burned CD mixes for each other. He would hop in my car, pop in a CD, and say, "I made this just for you," with a kiss on the cheek.

We both loved music, me more into the Top 40, while he was into rappers like Lil Wayne or Twista. Our relationship grew easily since we never fought, as life can be pretty seamless as teenagers in a small town. I told myself, *I am the luckiest girl in the world.* While I had previous high school relationships, none of them felt like this.

Senior year was highly anticipated since we would be the oldest kids on campus, ruling the school, dominating the volleyball court, and setting a more friendly tone for the school than the grades before us. My class of 2005 had been one of the most talented, smart, and athletic groups that our small private school had seen in a while, and the teachers would remind us of that often. We were the favorites, with little drama and a lot of exceptional athletes and artists.

The fall would bring about classes, homework, sports, and other extracurricular activities, and I was excited for it all with Zach by my side. Once school was back in session, Zach was immersed in football season, and I was busy with volleyball. Some school nights, when neither of us had too much homework, he would invite me over to his house, which I would otherwise naturally drive by on my way home. Sometimes, the busy evening only had time for a quick stop to say hi, sealed with a goodnight kiss.

I would attend his home football games wearing his letterman jacket; he was a standout tight end on the team and was only a sophomore. After the games, strangers would walk up to me and tell me how amazing my boyfriend was at football. He was a stud athlete, just like when I saw him that first day in the gym. He would also show up to my volleyball games and cheer me on. Once he was there, I would look up at him in the stands, and it was as if he had his eyes locked on me, waiting to catch my attention. He would then goofily wave at me and smile. I would acknowledge I saw him with a nonchalant hand and try not to allow a grin to light up my entire face.

Right around the time we met, I had gone to only a handful of parties. Once Zach's and my paths crossed, our time was spent together or excelling in sports, and he wasn't into drinking. Not that I was, but there was one time I drank alcohol, and my mom was called to come to pick me up. After that instance, my parents set some extreme rules going forward. But now, I was dating Zach, and I guess you could say he kept me on the straight and narrow. When Zach and I were together, my life felt complete.

3

Seal My Fate

Zach was playing a football game out of town, so I decided to attend a home football game with some of my friends. We were out in front of the school property where we decided to shotgun a beer in the car before going into the game. I guess you could say we were trying to keep things interesting.

Once we walked in, I was immediately grabbed and pulled aside, where I was caught up on the drama. Being that I was co-captain of the volleyball team, some classmates approached me to divulge that my middle hitter was stumbling in the side parking lot. Quickly, I and some other teammates went over to where she was. We made sure her friends were bringing her home and that she was out of sight as it was obvious she was intoxicated.

We walked back into the game and watched our classmates play under the Friday night lights. One of the Tinky Winkies was a cheerleader, and we mimicked the routines she did with touchdowns and holds. Home games were always fun, but in the midst of our cheering and laughing, I felt uneasy.

After the game was over, a handful of us went down to the river and the eeriness of the evening continued. After the commotion right before the game, the night didn't go as I had envisioned it would. I felt as though I was there more as an observer or bystander, watching the others drink and have a good time more so than being a participant. I sipped on one or two beers with my friends and teammates but had too much on my mind to let loose and enjoy myself that evening.

On Monday, the two teammates I was down by the river with and I were immediately called into the office at school, one at a time. I had already caught wind that my middle hitter was in trouble for showing up drunk to the football game but was told "someone" went to the administration and dropped our three names as well, insisting we were part of the problem and should also be suspended. That cheap-tasting beer I had that night did not taste good enough for what was ahead of me.

I stepped into the office by myself, prepared to lie, which is exactly what I did when the interrogation began. The athletic director asked me to sit across from him and the principal. They were staring me down. There was a distinguishable coldness in the room. While both of them had always been kind and friendly toward me, this was serious business.

"We've been notified by another student that you smelled like beer at the football game. Did you drink alcohol at the game on Friday?" the athletic director asked.

"No," I responded.

The two of them exchanged glances.

The AD was actually one of my favorite teachers—someone I loved and respected. In normal circumstances, I would never have lied to him, but I felt I had no choice.

Next they referenced my middle hitter and how she was seen intoxicated by a number of witnesses. "Did you see her?" they asked.

"Yes." I responded, giving short answers providing little information.

"What happened when you saw her?" he asked.

"I made sure she was safe, and her friends were taking her home," I said.

"So you weren't drinking with her?" he asked, firing off another question.

"No. I saw her, then I went into the game," I answered.

"But you didn't show up having consumed alcohol prior to the game?"

"No."

"Are you sure of your answer?"

"Yes."

"But someone said you smelled like beer at the game."

"I didn't drink anything beforehand," I lied.

There was a long pause before he spoke again. "Your two other teammates left the office admitting that they drank on Friday. Other students confirmed you arrived at the game all together. Were they drinking and you weren't?" he asked.

Was he lying and saying they admitted it to get me to confess?

I didn't know. I wasn't sure. All I was sure of is I'm not a liar and he could probably hear the uncertainty in my voice with every answer I gave. Maybe he had already confirmed (from them or elsewhere) information that proved my guilt.

Given the steady barrage of questions, I wondered if they planned to keep me in the office *until* I confessed. I crumbled under the pressure. This wasn't me. I started crying.

"It's okay, Heidi," he said in a consoling manner.

After a number of loud sobs, I replied, "No, it's not. My parents will move me to California," I blurted through tears.

"It's okay. I'm sure they won't move you to California," he assured me.

Sounds pretty drastic, right? I told you how my parents seemed to have a higher level of strictness and more severe repercussions for my actions than what felt like every other high school kid.

Well, for a few years, my dad had been itching to move out of Lynden. He owned his own company and considered relocating to North Carolina for a moment in time. We took a family trip to the East Coast and visited the campus of a local private high school.

Once he decided against North Carolina, he went in a completely different direction. My dad had grown up in Southern California when he was young and still loved palm trees and In-N-Out Burger. So instead, he decided that would be his big move. With my two older sisters already away at college, it was only me still at home, trying to fend for myself for my final semesters of high school to stay living in Lynden.

He had flown me down to California a few times and tried to get me linked up with girls in my grade at the private school in an attempt to convince me to move. Being a part of my close-knit group of Tinky Winkies and having a boyfriend I was in love with, I didn't want to go (though I did concede that California was dreamy).

Impatiently, he moved by himself since I was a few semesters away from graduating, and he allowed me to stay to finish my senior year. Meanwhile, he was living in California but paying two mortgages, two gas bills, and for multiple flights between California and Washington, all for me. Since my parents were spending more money and extra effort on me staying in Lynden, the rule was if I disobeyed again, it would no longer be my choice, and I would move to California.

So my athletic director was wrong. I was allowed to finish my volleyball season, and then I would move and finish the remainder of my senior year at another school in a different state. It felt surreal. Here I was getting in trouble for something I rarely did, but I would be enduring the biggest consequence for my actions. The events of that night weren't anywhere near worth the result that came thereafter. I was embarrassed and I knew I let a lot of people down.

The school board determined that the other two girls and I were not permitted to participate in games for three weeks. Practices included us standing on the sideline while younger, less experienced players took our spots. During the games, we would have to sit up high in the stands and videotape the games for further analysis and future strategy since we weren't allowed to play. It felt like everyone in the gymnasium would shoot disapproving glances and whisper about us during the games. It was a long, grueling three weeks.

In my senior English class, we were reading and discussing Dante's *Inferno*, which is a part of Dante's poem *The Divine Comedy.* His writing served as an allegory to explain Dante's journey of his soul through the different levels of hell back toward a reunion with God. Our teacher wanted us to write a paper to compare and contrast an event in our life to a level of hell as described by Dante in his writing. While I desperately wanted to write about something else, my current life predicament of being kicked off the volleyball team was blatantly staring me in the face.

I couldn't think of another topic to write about that would satisfy the assignment. I was completely at fault: I had let my teammates, coaches, teachers, friends, and parents down. The event shook up my core beliefs about myself: that I was a great friend and a good volleyball player. Without these parts of me, I wasn't sure who I was, and if the dreams I previously had for myself, like to receive a volleyball scholarship and play in college, would still hold true. I blamed myself that I would be leaving my life in my little hometown behind and felt like I was labeled a "bad kid." It didn't matter if other kids were drinking or not; what mattered was I was the one who got caught.

Knowing I had only days left at my high school, I was busy with late-night volleyball practices before our final big games were to be played at district and state now that I was allowed back on the team. I also made it to some of Zach's home football games and had a few last nights hanging out with friends. Not giving the paper much time, I threw together a brutally honest response for the task at hand, turned it in on a Friday, and completely forgot about it over the weekend.

Back at school on Monday, I was sitting in class where our English teacher was explaining how displeased he was with the effort put in on the paper. He said the majority of the class did a very poor job fulfilling the assignment and would be required to rework their writing and turn it back in.

Great, I thought.

He started passing back our graded papers and placed mine on my desk face down. I slowly picked it up and turned to the back page. There I saw my score: 100 percent, with a note that said, "This was an amazing comparison, honest and insightful. This story needs to be told."

But the reality was, it *wasn't* told. I made a point to avoid telling the details of it all to anyone. While it may sound like it's now written effortlessly in this book, it was never talked about in my day-to-day life. Although kids at school knew I had to take a three-week hiatus from the team for breaking code, aside from them, not a lot of people in my hometown nor down in California knew the reason why I would be moving. They believed it was because of my dad's business relocating, which was only part of the truth.

I didn't need constant sunshine nor the glamor or perception of "living the dream" in California. What I wanted were my friends, my boyfriend, and my simple small town existence. With everything up in the air, I went from living an easy and predictable life to freefalling into the unknown.

We had a chance to get first place that year, and although my middle hitter was completely off the team regardless of the decisions I made that one night, I couldn't help but think that had that evening never happened, we could have placed first instead of fourth in state. And it was all my fault.

Goodbye

The Tinky Winkies threw me a going away party two days before I flew to Southern California. It felt surreal to have all my friends show up at a "goodbye party" to say goodbye to me. *How was* I *the guest of honor?* I would be leaving the town I'd lived in since the moment I could walk, leaving the same group of kids I attended school with since kindergarten, leaving my five best friends and my first love, and leaving with no plans to move back.

Erika compiled a memory book of photos and notes, asked teachers to write me letters, and had a lot of classmates sign the book, many of whom I had known since I was five years old. It was bursting at the seams with seventeen years of love and memories to take with me; it was also impressive how put together it was when the news of my moving didn't allow her much time.

While at the party, and as written in the scrapbook, a lot of friends mentioned how much they would miss me and assured me that they would come down and visit. Since California is a destination location with beaches and sunshine, that wasn't too surprising to hear. However, it was my core group of girlfriends, the Tinky Winkies, this held true for, along with Zach and my friend Lucas.

Since I was the guest of honor and would be staying until the end of the party, I walked Zach out to say goodnight. The air was cold that November, gearing up for winter. I shivered in my Hollister track jacket and zipped it all the way up.

He stopped me next to his truck and wrapped his long gangly arms around me, first warming me up and then squeezing me tight. Tears welled up in my eyes. To alleviate the sad moment, he declared, "I love you more than you love ketchup."

We both laughed as I wiped a tear from each cheek.

"I'll see you in a few weeks!" I reminded him. I would be returning for the winter formal in December.

He leaned down, gave me a kiss goodnight, and said goodbye.

The next day was my last day at the school I had gone to since I was five years old. A lot of friends said goodbye at my party, and the rest of them did that day. I somberly walked the halls for my last time as a student. Before walking out the door, I had a prolonged hug with my friend Lauren in the hallway. We were both ugly crying with mascara running down our faces amidst our tears. We had been inseparable since the fifth grade. I knew she was irreplaceable.

I got in the car with my mom, holding my "goodbye book" as I waved to my friends, my school, and my life in this little town. I opened up the pink memory book to take a peek at Zach's note. He wrote in two separate spots. One was a lighthearted message full of inside jokes, and the other filled an entire page, saying how much he loved me, would miss me, and that I was his best friend. I closed the book and more tears rolled down my face.

That evening, I stayed the night at my cousin's house in Seattle, flew to California the next morning, and would start at my new school the following day. My dad, mom, and I would all live together in California.

Years later, when discussing these events with my mom, the only key factor she added to what I missed in my story was when I got in her car after school that day, en route to California, I gripped that pink *Creative Memories* book with both hands criss-crossed tight to my chest, with no intention of letting it go.

I didn't let a lot of things go.

4

"Life In the OC"

A plaid skirt, closed-toed flats, and a polo with an official school emblem. After attending the same school with a class of one hundred students since kindergarten, I found myself at a new high school in another state and weather regime with a mandatory daily attire: a school uniform.

"Hi! My name is Heidi. I am in the senior class, and I am the 'new girl.'"

This was a role I had never had before. Nervous is oftentimes a popular adjective to describe someone's first-day feelings when starting a job, attending a book club for the first time, or going on a blind date. *Will they like me? Will I embarrass myself? What if I hate it?*

Yet I didn't feel an ounce of nervousness when I walked in on that first day. I was resentful and determined to get it over with.

While my attitude may sound detached and pessimistic, I am, quite frankly, the opposite in its entirety. This was a decision I had not willfully made for myself, yet my actions drove my destiny. I had zero interest in putting myself out there to meet someone new, make a friend, or to even engage in a pleasant conversation. I was simply going through the motions.

I glanced at the school map I was handed of the Pacific Academy campus, along with my schedule. I easily found my first period classroom on the opposite side of school and was looking for my homeroom, where I needed to report to next. Once the bell rang, I packed up my Roxy book bag, stepped outside into the sunshine, and discovered I was only a few steps away.

From the get-go, my new school felt very different from what I was used to. It had no hallways, and all the kids were in uniform. We walked to and from class outside, which makes sense since they have sunshine year-round. The uniform polos the students wore all displayed the same PA emblem. Some of the girls paired the polo with the classic plaid skirt, which was exactly what I imagined a school uniform to look like.

I approached the open door to my homeroom, glanced down at my paper, and looked up to confirm the number next to the door matched. As I stepped inside the room, I was greeted with, "Heidi! It's so great to see you! How was your first class?"

His words were paired with a prolonged hug. I received a warm welcome with open arms from a familiar face. More questions followed, which I cannot recall. The students who were already sitting at their desks stopped mid-conversation to look at me with their questioning gazes. Even though I was wearing the same school uniform as them, I was a new face.

Ironically enough, my new homeroom teacher, the man asking all the questions, had been my PE teacher and soccer coach in the junior high at my old school in Lynden. He, too, had since then moved to Chino. Both Lynden and Chino were heavily populated by Dutch dairy-farming families. You can play "Dutch

Bingo" with a random Dutch person you meet, because if you're Dutch and they're Dutch, the odds of you knowing the same person are extremely high. Living in this new state with palm trees and constant sunshine made it feel odd that some of my new classmates lived on dairy farms and also listened to country music just like the kids did back home.

After his chitchatting, I walked down the aisle about three-quarters of the way and sat down. Once the bell rang and everyone filed into the room, the students needed a bit of coaxing to take their seats. As everyone calmed down, my old teacher took time to introduce me. This encouraged everyone to turn around at their desks and stare at me while he talked. I put a smile on my face yet, meanwhile, had a gaping hole in my heart.

My move and the resulting high-school transfer started the beginning of my double life. Not a double life where I had two different personalities or two different families like you might see on an eerie *Lifetime* Original Movie. Nope. I had a full-blown wonderful life up in Washington State that I was plucked from, hypothetically kicking and screaming, and now, here I was, the new girl at a new school, starting over from scratch.

Every day kept me feeling as though I was starring in a movie: the scenarios I was a part of, the drama that played out, how my life continued to go back and forth from one life setting to the other with a full list of characters, a wide range of emotions, drastically different scenes, and nonstop climatic events.

This is when I first developed the desire to write a book. Living two different lives in separate locations full of independent storylines continued to leave me feeling torn. I was uncertain which location I was meant to be in at any given moment, and all the while, I blamed myself.

Don't get me wrong; once living in SoCal, I didn't completely avoid people. After the initial shock of my first day and my new reality I had to come to terms with, I was cordial and made friends at school quickly. Some girls looked me up and down (and *still* treated me like dirt years later at our ten-year reunion, which says far more about them than me), but the majority of my classmates actually wanted to talk to me. I think it helped that I was a starter on the basketball team, and my new teammates vouched for me from the get-go.

I was quickly filled in on the past drama the following week. Like how one of the guys in the senior class kissed just about every girl in school. I was surprised by this information because the guy wasn't even that cute and was surprisingly short for how many girls were crushing on him. The history shared with me was convoluted with details about all the cool kids in the junior and senior classes. I kept imagining a large poster board in my head with everyone's picture on it, drawing imaginary lines from face to face to keep track of the connected and very tangled web. After attending the same school back home for the entirety of my life, the backstory never seemed this complicated.

After what felt like another three long weeks of my life at my new school, I was back on a flight home to attend a dance with Zach and the Tinky Winkies that December. It felt confusing to be departing for what someone might label as a weekend getaway, yet I was flying back to where I still referred to as "home."

Back in my hometown, five of us girls paired up with boys from the public school for the winter dance. We all got ready together for the evening, took pictures, and once at the event, it felt like I was constantly saying hi to everyone in proximity to me while on the dance floor.

You may be aware of the popular show on TV during the early 2000s called *The OC*. This was how everyone back home envisioned my new California life. They would ask about how glamorous it was and how wonderful it must be to live in endless sunshine. I would half smile and respond with, "Yeah! It's good . . . but I miss home." I couldn't kick the feeling that I was missing out on my highly anticipated senior year with my boyfriend and friends.

My arms were around Zach and his around me the entire evening, and I wouldn't have wanted it any other way. We were together, and that's what mattered. The first slow dance started to play, and he pulled me in close and whispered, "I've missed you."

My heart fluttered. I felt relieved. I hadn't a clue how long we would live apart and all I wanted was this: to be back in his arms.

"I've missed you, too! But I'm here! It's like I never left," I assured him.

But he was right. I had been missed and would continue to miss out on everything that I had been looking forward to. I was happy to be a part of the enchanting night with Zach and the girls, but it was unavoidable that I would fly back to California in a matter of hours.

My trips home never felt like enough time to be there. This first trip back, Lucas was so excited to have me home but was bummed about how the night unfolded since I didn't spend much time with him. He later told me that he disapproved of me dating

Zach because he thought I could do better. Every time I left, I had a flight booked to return to Lynden again, which always helped the leaving not feel so bad. I would say "See you later!" rather than the finality of a "goodbye." Knowing I had trips in my future was what kept me going in my new sunny reality.

It was hard to wrap my mind around it all. Most mornings, when I would wake up in my room in California, I would have to take a moment to remind myself where I was. I continued to fly back to my hometown and spend time with my friends and boyfriend; but, in reality, my life was here, thousands of miles away. I was a character living two different lives and disconnected in both. I was living in limbo, simply going through the motions. My heart had been shattered at the age of seventeen.

My New Normal

My first Christmas in California, we went to church as a family early in the morning and to Starbucks right after. We sat outside in a sizeable cement courtyard underneath large palm trees, with the sun gleaming down on my pale skin. We were surrounded by other restaurants closed for the holiday. In the center of the courtyard, there was a massively gorgeous Christmas tree decorated with large, colorful red, green, silver, and gold ornaments. We sat and enjoyed our iced coffees and reminisced about old Christmas memories.

I couldn't get over how this was my new normal and how off it felt. It used to be that every winter, we would pray for snow. It was hit or miss in the wintertime back home, but over the last few years, we were lucky enough to get some snow days. We would wake up early in the morning to listen to the radio station where they would announce all the school closures. If we didn't have school, we would spend the day sledding down the sloped sides of our house which led down to our large backyard, with lots of open space to make snow angels. Yet here I was, sipping a cold drink in eighty-degree weather on December 25.

I quickly learned that the best volleyball players in SoCal played club year-round. I tried out last minute and was placed on the top team in my age group at a local club. Most nights, I went straight from basketball practice to club volleyball, with tournaments on the weekends. This allowed little free time for anything else. But after applying to many of the private schools in California, I received a volleyball scholarship to a local private college where I would enroll after graduation in the fall.

My commute to my new high school was longer than just across my seven-square-mile hometown. It was on my drives to and from my new school or club practices where I would allow myself to cry. It cut my heart too deep to listen to any of my mixed CDs because the songs would transport my mind back "home."

Days after I moved, Kelly Clarkson released her album and song "Breakaway." I had it on repeat in my car and would turn the volume up to the max, listening to the words that seemed to be written for me to try to desensitize my heart.

Before the drastic move during my senior year, I had plans to go on a trip with Lauren and her family over spring break. My parents still allowed me to go, so I essentially had two spring breaks that year. Next was prom, senior ditch day, and grad night at Disneyland. *These California kids sure have it good,* I thought to myself. Then I realized, *I* am *one of those California kids now.*

So I guess that meant I had it good. While the daily tasks of school, practice, and club all felt like a standstill, time also sped by so quickly.

I ended senior year at my new school being voted "Most Friendly." Funny how that turned out. When I arrived mid-semester, I had no intention or agenda to make new friends. It was nice to know others saw me in that light, even though I felt as though I was a fish out of water. But after I warmed up to my new school, I was inherently myself and made the best of what I felt was my sad situation.

It made me smile when, a year or so later, one of the guys started to say, "Heidi, remember during sophomore year . . ."

Laughing, I cut him off and corrected him, "No, I don't! I transferred in senior year!"

I was added to the mix at the tail end, but to some of them, it felt as though I was there all along. No matter what façade I walked in with that first day, maybe it hadn't been so bad after all.

Split

I flew back home to watch my friends graduate from high school. It felt unnatural sitting in the grandstands watching my class walk the stage, shake hands with our principal, and move their tassel from right to left, with a diploma in hand, without me. I should have been up there with them in a long navy gown. It felt like I was watching a movie of someone else's life. I never would have dreamed for this moment to have gone the way that it did.

After the ceremony, I gave a lot of hugs and took pictures with my former classmates: them in gowns and me in street clothes. It still felt fresh and unsettling, but I smiled for the pictures anyway.

That night, the school put on an evening cruise to celebrate the senior class and allowed me to join. It was nice to be a part of it.

The next evening, I went to Zach's, and being together felt as though I never left. While he had a conflict and couldn't attend my graduation back in California, he and his brother would fly down for a visit later that summer. It became routine: we said goodbye, sealed it with a kiss, and continued our long-distance relationship.

Days after watching my friends graduate, the Tinky Winkies road-tripped down to watch me walk across the stage at my new high school and meet my friends.

After the girls returned home, the excitement of graduation and corresponding events calmed down. It was mid-June, and I would be reporting to college the first week of August for the volleyball team. With no option to work in the berries, my parents told me if I wanted to go out at all the rest of summer, I needed to make some money. I applied everywhere with no call-backs.

Then a new job resistantly fell into my lap thanks to one of my cousins. He lived nearby and joined us for dinner one evening where the topic came up about me finding work. I'm not sure if he was trying to be helpful or just funny, but from the other side of the dinner table, he announced, "Hey, Heidi. I got lunch at Jack in the Box today. They're hiring."

I slowly looked up from my plate with the most intense *I hate you* glare and turned my head back slowly to take another bite.

Chewing, I could feel eyes upon me. I looked up to find my dad staring at me.

"What?" I responded, muffled, with my mouth full.

"Are you too good for Jack in the Box?" he asked.

Well, yeah, I thought.

His question turned into a ten-minute lecture which included the reminder that if I didn't find a job that summer, I wouldn't be allowed to do anything.

I *despised* my cousin.

A week later, I was employed at a brand-new Jack in the Box down the street from my house. Management knew I had to leave in a month for volleyball, but they were short-staffed and needed help with taking orders, making tacos and curly fries, and filling sodas for the drive-through customers. It was an easy job, and I actually enjoyed it aside from smelling like fast food after my shifts. This is when I learned how much Californians love ranch dressing.

Zach and his brother came down to visit me. His little brother and I had always been super close, and he felt like my own. It was only a few weeks before I would start college, and Zach would fly back home and finish high school.

So my double life continued.

5

A Quick Detour

"If you aren't happy here, you won't be happy anywhere." That is what my teammate's resident director told her at college toward the end of our first semester.

In August, our volleyball team arrived on campus before the majority of the other students for "double days," which is attending practice twice in the same day. It was nice to be some of the only students on campus prior to the first day of school, with a couple of pleasant run-ins with the women's or men's soccer teams. Right away, I had some great bonding moments with my new teammates. It was one of the only positive things I took away from that semester.

I imagined for myself a true college experience: freedom, fun social events, and meeting cool people. Yet my expectations were met with feeling as though I was a small child back at my Christian camp in junior high. There were *So. Many. Rules.* But even at camp, we had a candy drawer, got to drive Jet Skis, and had water fights with super soakers.

Basically, church camp as a child was more enjoyable than the college I was attending. At the school, you were required to attend church twice on Sundays, chapel three days a week, and take a religion class every semester on top of your normal classes. You also had to sign in every night. On the weekends, if you weren't staying in your dorm, you were required to let them know where you would be staying and a phone number for them to be able to reach you.

I felt confined and claustrophobic. My desire to play volleyball for four years wasn't big enough to keep me there. What got me through the rest of that semester was trips to the LA fashion district and Taco Bell for Cheesy Gordita crunches with one of my teammates. Our semester was focused on volleyball and listening to the new 50 Cent *Massacre* CD on repeat in my teammate's amped-up Honda Civic, off campus, of course.

In the middle of all the commotion of starting college and thereafter making plans to transfer, I was sitting on my bed in my dorm room trying to finish up some English homework when a new message appeared with a ding. It was Zach saying hi.

He had signed onto AOL Instant Messenger (AIM). I missed him every day but knew with the two years of high school he had left, moving back now wasn't an option.

He started the conversation with small talk, asking how college was going and how I was doing. I was always eager to hear from him. We were catching up for a bit since our conflicting schedules didn't usually allow us much time to connect while we were both back in season, but we somehow found some time to talk almost every day.

Above my dorm room bed hung twinkling lights illuminating the wall covered with photos of friends and family, including Zach. I caught myself staring at our photo from our winter dance as we were chatting. We were together, dressed up, looking so happy, and I wondered when the next time that would be the case again. But, as our AIM conversation continued, he started to message me about a girl I knew.

We've been hanging out lately, he shared.

I didn't know how to reply.

Then he sent another message after my lack of response.

I'm thinking of asking her out.

My heart sank. Even though I knew this moment was bound to come, it still stung. This was his way of ending things because I was a million miles away and he found somebody else.

Oh really? I replied.

Yeah . . . I wanted to make sure that was okay with you.

I took a long pause. He was literally asking for my permission to date another girl. I knew my feelings toward him shouldn't hold back his high school experience, but I thought we were meant to be together.

Of course. I typed it and quickly hit enter.

I didn't want to second-guess my answer. I knew I could not ask him to wait. I was the reason we were living separate lives, and I wasn't coming back anytime soon. So I guess that's when Zach and I broke up.

The Unknown

Once I mustered up the courage to leave my scholarship, my teammate and I both transferred out to different schools. While I didn't know my next step in life, it was a decision I knew I would undoubtedly never look back on with regret.

A few weeks later, my ex-teammate and I met for lunch, and she broke down crying, expressing how happy she was that I left with her. She said that without me by her side, she didn't know if she would have had the courage to leave on her own. The silver lining was that my short and disappointing semester at that college gave me a lifelong friend.

I considered taking a semester off, but on a whim, I applied to another small private university. I hadn't heard of the school before living in Southern California and playing them in volleyball. The school was nearby, tuition was affordable, and I didn't recall the volleyball team being snotty like some of the others were. The university accepted my application mid-semester. Before I knew it, I was attending my third new school within a little over a one-year span.

I was starting over again. I had been the new girl before, but this time, it felt totally different.

You see, only a semester ago, everyone was new to college in the freshmen class. When I moved in high school, I had sports to connect me to my teammates. But this time around, while there were other mid-semester transfers like myself, most of them were commuters and lived off campus. The university would put on events for us to get involved, but I would politely decline. I was going to my new school simply to check the boxes: to receive a Christian education to please my parents and a degree to make me viable in society. I had no expectations that my time there would warrant anything more.

I attended college with no set career in mind. I never received a 4.0 like both of my sisters, but I worked hard and consistently got As and Bs. I originally chose business as my major. While my dad had started his own company, and I really had no other careers that caught my interest, I had no specific path in mind. So a business major felt like the obvious choice.

Within the major, accounting classes were required. They felt pretty straightforward, and the homework hadn't been challenging.

Weeks into the semester, we had our first test. Once I had completed it, I stood up to turn it in and noticed I was one of the first in the class to finish. I placed my test face down on the front table. Sitting nearby, my professor glanced over and motioned for me to come talk to him. I walked over and leaned in to hear him.

"Have you ever considered being an accounting major?" he asked.

I smiled. "Not exactly," I responded.

"Well, you should," he said. "You understand the concepts and do very well in this class."

The smile was because I found it laughable for him to bring this to my attention. Both of my older sisters were also accounting majors. While marketing or sales seemed a bit more exciting to me, I figured why not major in accounting to allow me to have a better understanding for all the aspects of a business. So I changed my major.

Emptiness

While previously I built my confidence on the belief that I was a dependable friend, fun to be around, and a great volleyball player, once I moved, changed schools, and then transferred from one college to the next, my life felt fragile and volatile. The qualities or skills I had that gave me self-worth and the essence of me felt out of reach.

That semester, the people I would meet and the connections I made felt as though I was simply passing the time. While I was never crippled with intimidation from anybody, my confidence hit an all-time low, and imposter syndrome got the best of me.

I believed I wasn't good enough, that I was a bad kid after getting caught drinking and that I should simply accept my life as is. *Maybe I'm not any more special or had a bigger purpose than the girl next door.* While I appeared happy and laid-back on the exterior, my self-esteem was virtually nonexistent. I allowed others' opinions of me to weigh heavily on my decisions. I was 100 percent extroverted, and I needed people to love me since I no longer loved myself.

Once attending my new university, it didn't take long until I joined the party crowd. On any given weekend, I would receive multiple texts for different parties to hit up, whether it be friends from high school, college, or work. I had options and I loved it. It boosted my confidence that I was fun and others enjoyed my company. I would stay busy with these "friends" and hide in their acceptance to distract myself from the obvious turmoil I felt inside.

While I was a part of different groups of people, classmates, roommates, and previous teammates, I still felt alone. I was experiencing my own quiet crisis while others observed my outward expression of cohesiveness. So much changed in my life in a little over a twelve-month span, and so much felt out of my control. What I did have influence on was my status on campus. I liked being referred to as the "life of the party," and I wore the title proudly.

It was then that I habitually made poor choices. I once heard this period referred to as a "black hole." Some people might experience this era in their own life as a tattoo they regret, an abusive relationship they didn't leave, or a blow-out fight with a best friend or family member that destroyed the bond. In my case, I let my insecurity get the best of me, and it controlled my behavior. I would binge drink most weekends and would maintain my self-worth based on attention. I painted myself as the victim in my own story, and I let it define my life. I dyed my hair brown and started to gain the "freshman fifteen." When I saw my reflection in the mirror, I didn't even recognize myself anymore.

Just as I was trying to find the right friends, find myself, and find happiness again, I met a girl named Chloe. My life started to change in the right direction. Chloe exuded the epitome of what I was lacking: self-esteem.

6

Soulmate

I saw Chloe in between classes a few times. She was tall, skinny, and blonde, and she always wore cute clothes. It was kind of annoying.

Unbeknownst to me, we had a mutual friend who planned to come over to my on-campus apartment one evening. Prior to her arrival, she asked if she could invite Chloe. I responded to her request with an unenthusiastic "Sure."

The two of them arrived at my apartment: Chloe, in dramatic fashion. She stole the show and didn't stop talking for a good half hour after she arrived. We both knew of each other, but it was our first time acknowledging that the other existed. But during that half hour of time, while her reputation preceded her introduction, my opinion of her took a major turn.

Chloe was updating our mutual friend on her life. I was only half listening, but my ears perked up when I heard her touch on three topics: "My four best friends from home . . ." "I've been in love with him the last four years of my life . . ." and finally, "My life is so crazy; I just need to write my book."

This girl's words were my life.

In a very calm and cool way, I asked about the love of her life. I followed up my question by saying, "I'm curious because I, too, am still in love with my ex-boyfriend from high school."

She told me how her family was originally from the area, and in the summer, she would spend a fair amount of time down south with her cousin. She met a boy, and they hit it off in junior high. She, however, was from Northern California, so even though they lived apart, they dated for a few years. Since then, he found another girl and pretended like he was over Chloe entirely, but she was still hoping they would end up together as they were now attending the same college.

Her story was oddly similar to mine, but instead of how I moved away from the love of my life, she moved from being apart to being in the same city. Regardless, it was complicated and a constant love battle. I also told her I had a group of best friends back home and that I, too, wanted to write a book.

Once we were back at school after Christmas break, Chloe and I hung out again. We went over to her friend's place and were playing beer pong in the garage. I couldn't hold the seal any longer, so I went inside to use the bathroom. Well, next thing I knew, my phone rang, and while I was peeing, Chloe came into the bathroom doing her own emergency potty dance.

I picked up my phone.

"Where are you at?" It was my friend from the basketball team.

"I'm . . . in the bathroom?" I answered, not knowing the name of the host of the party whose house we were at.

Hearing other voices paired with commotion, he asked, "What are you doing in the bathroom?"

Laughing, I responded, "Taking a quick break, but we will be right back to playing beer pong soon."

"You're playing beer pong . . . *in the bathroom*?" He emphasized the second half of the question.

Once I was done, I pulled up my pants, and Chloe and I switched places for her turn. Just then, two more girls joined us. When I went to wash my hands, with my phone between my shoulder and ear and my friend still on the line, the water sprayed all over Chloe and me. I handed Chloe my phone, grabbed a blow dryer from under the sink, and turned it on.

That's when Chloe yelled, "Stop blowing me dry, Heidi!"

And just like that, our friendship was sealed. We have been inseparable ever since. With Chloe as my new friend, something shifted. I found someone I belonged to. This girl was my soulmate.

After another late night spent together, Chloe and I walked into Yum Yum Donuts around 1 a.m. It was about a mile from campus. Looking up at the menu, I knew I wanted a donut but was deciding if I should get a Frappuccino in addition to the already unnecessary splurge or if I should skip coffee altogether at that hour.

We were the only customers in the shop, so we continued our discussion about boys and how lame they were. Once we were ready to order, the guy behind the counter kept smiling and was stifling his laughter. Chloe and I exchanged confused glances, and I asked him, "What's so funny?"

"It's just—" he said, faltering as he thought about what to say next, "you're both way too pretty to let any guy get you down."

Chloe and I laughed. "Aww . . . thank you!" we replied in unison.

We grabbed our items and walked out of the donut shop. Chloe turned to me and exclaimed, "Wow, the advice you receive from Yum Yum in the wee hours of the morning is priceless."

But he was right. What was I missing that made my life feel so terrible? Was it Zach? Was it no longer playing volleyball? I had lost the things that once built my confidence, and now, it was just me. Unknowingly, my identity was based on the culmination of others' opinions of me rather than who I was on the inside.

Later that semester, Chloe and I went through a Starbucks drive-through together. The barista said, "Hey! I know you two. You go to my school; you're Chloe and Heidi."

We looked at each other and grinned.

"*Yeaahh*!!" we responded. We started feeling like our duo was pretty cool.

If we weren't dillydallying around our city, one of our favorite things to do was pack up and drive to San Diego. We both felt as though that place was magic.

One weekend we decided to head down, Lucas from Lynden was also in San Diego, visiting his best friend. We joined groups for a fun-filled time. San Diego became a meaningful place for us and a getaway when we wanted to shake up the ordinary.

Dock

Spring break, sophomore year, we set out for the river late one night. This trip was a bit smaller group of friends than the norm. Oftentimes, we would cram a bunch of people into the river house, with someone crashing on the massive bean bag and another on a blow-up mattress in the larger-than-normal laundry room. The river house in Arizona was owned by our friend's dad. It was located on the water with its own dock across from an island with a no-wake zone.

The first night we arrived, we played beer pong, listened to music, and learned how to booty pop. There was no shortage of laughter the entire evening.

After spending the next day on the water, wakeboarding and cliff jumping, the boys took a taxi to the casinos that evening while the girls stayed in. Chloe and I threw on sweatshirts to go down on the dock while our friend showered then mixed drinks for us upstairs. We held tight onto the railing walking down; I was sure to watch my step, as the house provided little light by the water for us to tiptoe in the shadows down to the dock. On the other side of the river was a highway, creating a large open space, with the sounds of the moving river and occasional brave souls passing by on the water late at night.

While Arizona gets super hot in the summertime, we were there in early April, allowing for cooler evenings. As we lay down on the dock, our eyes adjusted to the darkness and we could see the river flowing by. The sky was so clear you could see every single star out that night.

"Wow, look at the stars! This is incredible!" I exclaimed.

"Well, this is Arizona," Chloe replied. "It sure isn't California with all the smog."

"Yeah, but I grew up in Washington and only remember seeing stars this vivid and clear during a meteor shower."

"Well, isn't that because it's cloudy and rainy all the time up there?"

She had a point.

I couldn't look away from the dark sky covered in what looked like bright speckles of confetti scattered everywhere. With our backs and bottoms on the dock, we chatted while looking for shooting stars.

Gazing into the universe that evening reminded me how small I was . . . that whatever problem I was currently facing may not be as insurmountable as it seemed. My life relentlessly felt as though I was on a merry-go-round. It was moving quickly with trips back home and a busy schedule at college, but it wouldn't stop for me to hop off and take a break. It was fun and even felt surreal at times, yet I was missing *something*. But what was the problem? We were two girls having fun in college: We would start our partying on Thursday (or "Friday Jr." as we now call it) and always had something going on every night into the weekend. We kissed guys but didn't like any of them since we were both stuck on our first loves. But, in retrospect, maybe that was a blessing in disguise. It helped keep us occupied from wandering into new feelings or territory.

After a prolonged silence, I confidently said, "I think I'm a pizza."

Chloe laughed. "What?" she asked. Maybe the Arizona sun had already gotten to me.

"Yeah. It's as though I'm a pizza, right? I have great toppings: I'm social, so that's the pepperoni; I think I'm relatively down to earth, that's some spicy and delicious sausage; I'm fun, so we can add some pineapple; athletic, which could be a bit of basil to add to the freshness; and Zach and I are best friends and we've never had a fight—that's all the cheese. Therefore, I have the qualities—or toppings, rather—of the greatest and most delicious pizza. So why isn't he ordering his favorite pizza?"

"Exactly," Chloe responded. "You *are* his perfect pizza with everything he could possibly want on it. But you don't live near him, so he's not ready to eat his pizza yet. He's cooking the pizza and taking his time finishing school. He's casually keeping it in the oven for when he's ready, but this pizza is starting to burn."

"Yup," I said, "and nobody likes burnt pizza."

I wanted to move on. But I couldn't move past the feeling that he was the best I ever had. We had no issues in our relationship, and I was certain that no one better was out there. Our host walked down the ramp, impressively holding mixed drinks for all three of us and asked, "Wanna go skinny-dipping?!"

Summer of '07

After finishing my sophomore year of college, I was on a flight the very next day to spend the next four months in my hometown. I was thrilled to live with Lauren for the summer. The two of us never really had any arguments; she was always calm in nature, kind with her words, and considerate of my feelings. Others were often intimidated by her, likely because she was pretty and always seemed to have a boyfriend. But even after years passed, she was always there for me, just like she was back in grade school.

Anywhere I went in town, I saw someone I knew, and any evening event would turn into a mini high school reunion. There were a few nights where we would coordinate sleepovers with the Tinky Winkies, just like the good old days, complete with puppy chow and brownie batter. It was exactly what my heart needed and what I missed most. But, of course, while I was *finally* back in my hometown, Zach had a new girlfriend.

Lauren was dating one of Lucas's friends, which helped solidify the four of us being inseparable. You would think we had coupled off, but Lucas was dating someone who clearly didn't care for me much since he would often choose to spend his time with us. But Lucas had claimed the title of my "best guy friend" years ago. Plus, I was still in love with Zach.

Through knowing the right people, I got connected to working at the waterslides that summer. It was a seasonal job, and they needed lifeguards during the few months the sun was out. The head of maintenance was Lauren's family friend, and he hooked me up with the easy task of cleaning the pools each morning, patrolling the park during the day, covering for the lifeguards at lunchtime, and getting paid to enjoy the Pacific Northwest in its finest months of the year.

One early evening during off hours, he let us explore the park by ourselves and ride the waterslides. Lauren; her boyfriend, Lucas; a few other friends; and I broke all the rules going down the big slides: not spacing ourselves; holding onto each other, creating long chains; or going down headfirst. It was one of those moments where time stood still. Despite the sun setting, I was having a carefree summer with old friends and wishing it all would never end.

If I wasn't working at the waterslides, my days were filled with longboarding, bucking bales, meeting new baby chicks or puppies, riverbank sunbathing, floating down the river, bonfires, or sidewalk-chalking driveways from top to bottom. It was the ideal summer you would expect in a small town.

One day while hanging with the girls, we went to grab some food and had to drive to the other side of town. We all piled into

Erika's jeep with the music turned up loudly. I noticed she took an unexpected route (which I thought was out of the way), then turned down Zach's street. I figured she just wanted to make the joyride a bit longer, as it was a gorgeous day and our hair was blowing in our faces riding in the jeep with the top down. As we approached his house, she turned the song on her iPod to Avril Lavigne's "Girlfriend."

"*No*!" I instinctively blurted out. "Please turn it down!!"

Erika shouted back at me, "This isn't from you, this is from me! Just let it happen!"

Zach's house was on a block all on its own in the middle of town. She drove by, turned, then went back around the house two times. I couldn't stop my uncontrollable laughter.

Erika always had my back. The song was about how Avril didn't approve of her ex-boyfriend's new girlfriend. I worried if he or his family, or, even worse, the new girlfriend, would hear the song, so I preemptively covered my face as a shield from revealing my identity. I felt embarrassed, yet, simultaneously, I loved every minute of it.

Big Plans

A few weeks later, my middle sister came to visit after she had spent an interim period in Spain. She was inspired and still buzzing from her time spent abroad. She encouraged me, saying, "Heids, you *have* to study in Spain!"

I had heard nothing but amazing things from others who went abroad, but it sounded like it would take a lot of effort to pull off. I had *just* coordinated my summer back home. I had been looking forward to a summer with my girls, but I would be lying if I didn't admit how disappointed I was that Zach was dating someone else. Here I was, where I thought I needed to be, and I *still* wasn't content. I thought living here would bring comfort to the whirlwind of my past few years, yet Zach threw a wrench in my high hopes and made the summer bittersweet. So, despite being "home," there was still an uneasiness inside that was hard to ignore.

I contemplated what my sister said and considered the fact that I only had two years left of college. After an unconventional senior year in high school, I was committed to avoid another split year. That left me with the only option of going abroad my junior year, which was quickly approaching.

"Well, I can try!" I responded.

"It's my biggest regret not studying abroad for a whole semester. I'm lucky to have spent a few weeks there for my class. I know you can pull it off!" she said.

Once my sister assured me that Sevilla was the place to study, I never considered another location. The seed was planted.

The wheels in my head started turning. A semester abroad sounded incredible. Maybe those exquisite landmarks and surroundings would help me move past my uncertainty with myself. Maybe it would help me get over Zach, or I might meet someone entirely new. I wasn't quite sure if I could make it happen with my major, but after some research and comparison of courses, my university honored my chosen abroad program.

I was going to Spain.

Part 2

A true artist is not one who is inspired,
but one who inspires others.

—Salvador Dali

7

España

"Why would you study abroad?" My college roommate questioned my plans. "You're going to miss *everything*!"

I chose to smile and not respond since I knew I was going to enjoy far more amazing things in Europe that next semester than I would in my college town. Living abroad wasn't something I had ever envisioned for my life, and I was stoked for the extraordinary opportunity.

Once I let Lucas know I was leaving for Spain, he and a friend drove down at the last minute to say goodbye to me before I left that January. Since he had been coming down almost every three months, he wouldn't have any impromptu visits until I would return home. Lucas always looked for an excuse to visit, but he also supported me with all my big dreams.

We made plans to meet up in Huntington Beach to say goodbye, and one of my friends tagged along. After Lucas left with his buddy, my friend turned toward me and said, "Lucas, for sure, loves you!" I mean in a weird way I knew he did, but only as a friend. Everyone knew who my unabating love was for.

Sevilla: No Me Ha Dejado

As our plane touched down in Madrid, I pulled up the window shade as the sun set in my new country. Everything looked different, but it felt exhilarating. I would soon be immersed in a culture distinct from what I was accustomed to. I didn't know a single person in my program, and I would be spending the next five months of my life here. I was ready for it. I was ready for adventure.

Once I tracked down my two large suitcases stuffed with clothes for the semester in baggage claim, I was picked up from the airport by a chaperone from my program. I arrived at my hotel room, dropped my bags, and met up with a friend from my university back home who was also studying abroad for the semester in Madrid. That night, we were running through the streets of Spain giggling with excitement to be together, be abroad, and be looking at new experiences and opportunities every day. We went to a popular seven-story club called Capitol. There, I ordered my first drink at a bar at the age of twenty. She ordered a mojito, so I joined her. Rookie surprise, but when handed the beverage, I was oblivious to the fact that a drink would contain leaves.

I laughed at my ignorance. "Cheers to a semester in Spain!" I said. We "jinxed" in unison and clinked our glasses to kick off the promising months ahead.

At the time I studied abroad, the internet wasn't available everywhere like it is now. I had to purchase credits and download Skype on my computer to call family and friends. I and a lot of my new classmates bought Spanish phones called Vodafone to text each other. My communication back home was scarce aside from updating my parents on how I was doing and where I was traveling.

Since I was busy planning trips every other weekend, I didn't engage much with anyone back home. Zach would leave me messages on MySpace that I rarely made time to respond to. I would have to log onto the internet at cafes, use the biblioteca at school, or sit in my cold cell-like room at my homestay on my laptop instead of enjoying the Spanish life outside of those concrete apartment walls. The time difference also made it less of a priority for me, as it was more challenging than engaging. I would log on and read messages from Zach that typically included: *Wow. Amazing. I miss you. Hope you're having a great time*, always signing his messages with, *Love, Zach*. I would often send back short replies. While I didn't reciprocate much in our communication, my feelings didn't fade.

Using my planning skills, I wrote out my homework for the semester and made to-do lists. I assured myself that since I was living in Spain, I should try to go out every night to experience all that this European life had to offer. So I got my homework done ahead of time to always be available for fun. Whether friends asked to me to grab tapas, drink out of an eighty-Euro-cent cardboard carton of vino by the river, or go out dancing on the weekends around midnight at the club Buddha, I was determined to say yes to new experiences and make the most of being here. From siestas to starting the evening by going out at 10 p.m., the culture emphasizes enjoying food, family, and life.

I traveled to a lot of cities in Spain, and in each new place I went, there were cathedrals to tour, plazas to explore, and charming parks with fountains to enjoy. We would often have to make the choice between gelato or iced coffee (depending on how we were feeling that day) when the afternoon rolled around once everyone awoke from their siestas.

At my new school, in addition to my three business classes, I also took Spanish II and History of Spanish Art. I felt so connected to be immersed in the country where the history I learned about not only took place, but I could also go see it for myself in real life and not just read about it in books. We went to a bullfight, saw flamenco dancing, and got to view art by Picasso and Dali. We also visited structures designed by Gaudi, like the Sagrada Familia, Casa Batlló, and Park Güell, while in Barcelona. My Spanish was the best it's ever been as I could carry on and understand basic conversations with a complete stranger.

I took a long weekend trip to London, where one of my high school friends from California was studying abroad. I fell in love with London. It felt like a cold and dreary Seattle with British accents; it also felt like the home I knew.

After a few days there, we took the underground train to Paris, where we stayed for three nights. I made sure to eat three crepes each day with zero regrets since I had no set plans to return to France to enjoy the authentic cuisine.

One evening, while eating a crepe, we were caught off guard when the Eiffel Tower unexpectedly began to sparkle. It was ravishing. My life felt radiant. At that moment, I thought how remarkable it all truly was. The Eiffel Tower is an icon I had seen in books or in movies as a young child. I had no previous aspirations to go see it simply because I thought I never would. Yet here I was, watching it glisten in the frigid cold on a completely cloudless night, and it was magical.

That was one of the moments, among others, that solidified the notion that whatever it is I want in life, whatever dream I have, I can make it come true.

My middle sister took advantage of me living in Spain for the semester and came to visit. We traveled to Italy and Greece together during my spring break and took each day as it came with only a backpack in tow. We would explore the city we were in, and once we felt ready to move to the next one, we found the train station and had exquisite timing catching a train and continuing our trip.

We started in Milan, then traveled to Pisa, Venice, Florence, Cinque Terre, and Rome. From there, we took a quick flight over to Greece, where we saw the Acropolis and traveled to Mykonos by ferry. It was undoubtedly the spring break of a lifetime.

Stars Align

I had a string of combined instances that were completely random yet reinforced that my life decisions were meant to be.

When we visited Cinque Terre, which is an area made up of five seaside villages along Italy's coastline, my sister and I completed the 7.5-mile hike that connects the five cities to one another and took our time exploring each one. It was a picturesque day, with views of the colorful buildings in each town overlooking the Ligurian Sea.

The sun began to set as we were seated on large boulders perched above the iridescent water at our fifth and final stop. Cooling air was settling in, so we decided to walk back to our hotel to arrive home before dark. We carried our shoes as the sand squished between our toes.

We passed a couple with their daughter running close behind them, and we continued walking. Then, a few seconds later, I heard, "Heidi?"

I turned around. It was a familiar face from Lynden. While home that previous summer, I hung out with this aunt of my friend a few times when we were at her grandma's house. My friend was the same teammate that was kicked off the team with me for three weeks back in high school.

"Hi!" I responded. "Oh my goodness, how are you? I didn't know you were traveling to Italy!"

"My husband is here for work, and my daughter and I tagged along for fun. My daughter saw you and said, 'That's Heidi, that's the friend we met at Grandma's house!' I didn't believe her, but gosh, she was right. It is so random to see you!"

"You too!" I responded.

We chatted for a few more minutes, gave each other hugs, and were on our way. Had I not lived in Lynden that summer right before I left, and had I not studied abroad for the semester, this random moment, in the middle of Italy, would have never coincided.

Next, one of the closest friends I made while abroad (who was also in my same program) was from North Carolina. Toward the end of our semester and after spending a lot of time together, we started talking about life back home. I told her how, years ago, my dad was looking into moving to North Carolina and how one time, my sister and I toured a small school in the Greensboro area. As the conversation continued, she and I made the connection that the school I toured was the same private school she had attended since kindergarten.

What a coincidence! It felt as though this girl and I were absolutely destined to be friends, no matter what course life took to get us there.

My last random event happened after returning from abroad, when I ran into another classmate from Sevilla in Southern California.

All three instances felt bizarre and yet so divinely timed. What may seem like random and insignificant details made me feel connected to God's bigger plan through those intertwining surreal moments. It made me feel that maybe I was headed down the right path.

At the End of the Day

Studying abroad was hands down one of the best decisions I have ever made in my life. I moved to another country for five months, made friends, learned the language, and enjoyed my time on the other side of the world without anyone to lean on.

Living in Spain and traveling to other countries gave me the assurance that however I wanted my life to look like, wherever I wanted to live, I could make it happen. That the world is a huge place with so many people everywhere and ceaseless possibilities. It also helped me to appreciate all that I had in California and in Washington.

Yet this didn't mean I had run away from my inner turmoil. I was still me: unsettled and confused. I would be heading home, back to my torn scenario of life, and while the semester abroad was refreshing, eye-opening, and exhilarating, it didn't fix what remained off inside me, and I couldn't shake the feeling.

The Yearly Trip

As much as I grew up loving it, living in a small town also has its disadvantages.

After returning home from abroad, I had plans to take a trip to Lynden before starting my senior year of college. While I was in Spain, Lauren moved to a house on Second Street, directly across from Zach's house. How convenient.

Yet, once again, while I was there visiting, he was still dating that other girl. Figures. But I wasn't fazed because he would still call or text me and say he would "always be in love with me," that "no other girl could compare to me," and how he would keep "looking for me in other people but never find it." From the affirmations he gave me, I thought that, deep down, he would rather be with me. This was the story he continued to tell, and I continued to believe him.

As we passed Bellingham, only fifteen minutes away from my hometown, my phone rang. Back then, I paid for ringtones and picked different songs for my favorite people. The song "Vindicated" by Dashboard Confessionals rang out. I smiled and picked up and said, "*Heyy*! How's it going?"

It was Lucas.

"Where are you?" he asked.

"Don't worry, I'm on my way from Seattle. I should get in around 7 p.m. Everyone is going to New York Pizza," I said.

"Yeah, I know! I have to finish up work and I'll call you before heading over there," he replied.

"Okay, sounds good!" I answered.

"See you soon!" he said.

Lucas always made me smile. He was the kind of the guy you were super tight with but wouldn't try to pursue anything with for the fear of ruining your friendship.

Hours later, Lucas hadn't shown up at New York Pizza like he said he would. I had been preoccupied catching up with all the familiar faces at the pizza place and forgot he said he would be there.

We headed back to Lauren's, blaring music in her car and laughing about the events of the evening. At this point, I was a little delirious from my long day of travel and our late night out. Then I remembered how Lucas never showed up. It was so unlike him to not come when he said he would.

Right then, my phone rang. It was Lucas.

"Where are you?!" I asked, irritated.

"*Heidiii*, I'm so sorry! My car is in the shop, all my roommates wanted to go to sleep, so I didn't have a way to get to—"

Getting out of the car and cutting off his excuses, I asked, "Why aren't you here?"

"I'm sorry, you know I want to see you so bad . . ."

And in that instant, standing in the damp front lawn of Lauren's house, I stumbled into a muscular 6'1" young man who engulfed me in his arms. Of course, I knew exactly who it was: Lucas not only always had a way of redeeming himself, but he always made me feel special.

One time, when he was in SoCal visiting his friend, I received a text from him saying, *I'm so close to you. If I don't come see you, I know I'll regret it.*

So he showed up an hour later, stayed for an hour, and was on his way back down to San Diego. He had been on the road for longer than he was sitting in my apartment just to say hi.

That night, after he surprised me at Lauren's house, we kissed. Unexpectedly. As I fell fast asleep with him holding me in his arms, he whispered, "Maybe we should just be together."

The next morning, I slowly woke up when he gave me a half-hug goodbye. I heard the front door quietly close behind him.

When I saw Lucas later that week, nothing further was discussed. While my heart fluttered at his words, nothing was ever said. I knew his track record with girlfriends wasn't so good, and since he was my best guy friend, there was an obvious red flag. I knew I could never try to make us to be a "thing," for if we didn't work out, I would never forgive myself for trying. I absolutely needed Lucas in my life.

8

Blue Haven

Senior year of college took off with lightning speed. Five of us girls found the ideal house off campus, and Chloe eagerly claimed her title as our "sixth roommate."

Once a few days of classes passed, Chloe and I showed up at an off-campus party our first weekend with school back in session. I was eager to see everyone all together and catch up after being abroad the previous semester.

After chatting with some old friends, I made my way into the kitchen where a new face caught my eye. My mom would often use the phrase "tall, dark, and handsome" when referring to a good-looking man, and that described this guy to a T. He was wearing a hat that looked as though he stole it from Indiana Jones. Once we made eye contact, he grinned and asked, "And why don't I know you?"

Next thing I knew, the two of us were talking in the kitchen for over an hour. I learned he had transferred in to play men's volleyball while I was studying abroad. He flattered me with compliments and was constantly making me laugh.

The conversation went real deep, real quick. He was a go-getter: confident, intriguing, and great at prompting thought-provoking questions. I couldn't believe he had transferred in and no one told me!

I felt caught off guard and unprepared for what was next. Then he interrupted my thoughts with, "You're perfect. Can I marry you?"

Well, please don't get excited like I did. My heart ended up smashed in just a couple months. I was under the impression that we could be a good fit: he attended church with me and would even reach for my hand to hold during the sermon. Then there was another night I needed a few groceries and basic items for the house, and he came along just to spend time with me. What first seemed to be sincerely thoughtful and sweet times together turned into nothing but a dead end. Life and drama with this guy stole the first half of my senior year and took the wind out of my sails to try and find someone new. He thought we could still be friends while he was simultaneously seeing other girls, and I confidently told him no.

Fast forward to New Year's Day, when I chose to put the boy troubles out of my mind. The roommates and I were on the couch discussing how our only roommate not present was at her parent's house in Eastern Washington in multiple feet of snow. It sounded a lot dreamier than cleaning up the house after our New Year's party with sticky floors. Besides, I was still embarrassed about crying when the "Indiana Jones Hat Thief" showed up to our party uninvited.

Those first few days of the new year were likely the only time for the remainder of the year I had multiple days with no agenda and only one shift at work on the calendar. I was determined to make what was left of senior year memorable. So I blurted out my bright idea: "Guys, we should just drive to our roommate and play in the snow!"

Two hours and two phone calls to our jobs later, we were on our way on the most spontaneous road trip of our lives in the dead of the worst winter the Pacific Northwest had seen in years. After multiple instances of almost turning back around to go home, we made it to Seattle. It felt different to get to the city, then hang a right toward Eastern Washington instead of heading north to Lynden.

Late that night, we traveled through Stevens Pass. It had just opened back up that afternoon, even with the ongoing snowfall. We were all awake, wide-eyed, watching the snow hit our windshield and the road in front of us. Suddenly, we hit a patch of ice on the two-lane highway, and our car went into a spin in the middle of the night. My roommate, whose turn it was to drive, strategically pulled the emergency brake and we luckily stopped in our lane with the nose of our sedan pointed in the correct direction. We all looked at each other and let out a sigh of relief.

In that same moment, a semi went zooming by in the lane right next to us. We were stunned that our car happened to come to a halt at the precise angle that we were safe and a collision was averted.

Right then, a white rabbit randomly hopped across the highway in front of us. I felt in my heart it was a symbol from God, confirming He was keeping us safe.

Over twenty-six hours and more than a thousand miles later, we arrived at our destination. We spent four snow-filled days with our roommate and her family. After our memorable time spent together, some snow had melted, making our journey back home much more safe. Even though it may have seemed completely irrational to drive a car with no four-wheel drive through the snowy mountains, it was a risk we were willing to take for the thrill of the adventure. I hadn't lost my appetite for excitement or spontaneity after all, and I sure wasn't going to let a guy get me down. Senior year was indeed looking up.

Yoga

My roommate and I worked a part-time job in the marketing department for a car dealership during college. Our boss gifted us a basket complete with snacks, wine, and a yoga DVD for all our hard work.

We popped in the DVD to try the class but couldn't stop laughing during the poses. The teacher instructed us to "be one with the earth" among other "woo-woo" imperatives.

After watching the video and attempting to follow along as best we could, we poured ourselves the bottle of Riesling that had also been in the basket, sprinkled in some raspberries, and sat on the couch to chat as the class continued to play in the background.

After that first yoga experience, a friend of mine told me about hot yoga and how she heard that "fat melts right off of your body." I thought I could use a little help in that area and that this might just do the trick. I googled hot yoga only to find that the search populated results for "Bikram yoga." Reading further, I found that a brand-new studio had opened a month earlier near my parents' new house in Orange County. The studio offered a two-week intro pass for $29. I was curious to try it and was determined to get the most bang for my buck, wanting to attend as many classes as possible during that two-week span to see if I could actually see results.

Days later, I arrived at the studio. I placed my items in a locker right when a gorgeous and fit lady who looked as though she was in her forties—and had a body I was striving to attain in my twenties—asked, "Is it your first time here?"

Was it so obvious?

"Yes, it is!" I responded.

"Oh, you're going to love it," she assured me.

Losing weight was my priority. Enjoying it would be a huge plus.

As I entered the heated room, I chose an open spot right in the middle of the large space relatively close to the instructor's podium but not quite the back row. Within minutes, a tiny brunette (our teacher) opened the door, flicked on the lights, and entered the room while greeting the class. She had an inviting warmth about her; that was in addition to the insane heat.

Time spent in there felt like eternity. But I knew I could put my game face on and endure tough workouts as long as there was an end in sight. This, however, was the longest ninety minutes I had ever encountered, and I relentlessly fought my urge to leave the room and my desire to breathe "normal air."

I made it to the final *savasana*. This is the last posture where you lie down on your back with your arms and legs positioned close to your body, and you are encouraged to close your eyes for the first time during the class. It's typically the posture to seal the end of most yoga practices, enabling maximum relaxation. It allows for a final deceleration of your heart rate and gives you a moment or two to catch your breath and embrace your clear mind before stepping outside of the yoga room and back into the world.

I was drenched in sweat. After a few others got up and started to leave, I followed them to the locker room to shower. Once finished, I grabbed my things to head out the door but was stopped by that same friendly lady from before class.

"So did you like it?!" she eagerly asked.

Caught off guard and very bad at lying, I replied with an overly enthusiastic, "Uh, yeah! It was good!"

"Great," she replied. "Make sure to drink lots of water and you'll get amazing sleep tonight. Then come back and take another class as soon as you can."

I was unsure how I truly felt. I was thrilled to make it out alive and breathe the outside air I had been eagerly waiting for. But I wondered why that class had been packed full of people. How did they *all* like it so much? It was as if everyone in that room knew something I didn't.

Walking to my car, I felt a nudge inside of me. Something happened in that ninety minutes, and I wasn't quite sure what it was or how to explain it, but I felt free. Maybe it was the clearing of my mind, accomplishing a hard task, or sweating every last ounce of perspiration from my body as if I was wrung out like a sponge.

Already, I knew I wanted to go back . . . maybe to improve my postures or even to combat my mind that told me throughout class that I wasn't good enough to make it through. I felt the detox to my body and a calming peace in my soul.

Predictable

The next month, I told Chloe that Zach was coming to visit. He was back to being single and telling me how in love with me he would always be.

I asked Chloe if she wanted to come with me to pick him up at the Los Angeles Airport. She obliged. We had purchased Taylor Swift's new album and wanted to listen to the whole thing from start to finish. Taylor always had a way of speaking the words we didn't know our hearts felt. Chloe was obsessed with the fifth song "White Horse" on the album, and we were almost to her favorite one.

I had recently gotten a new flip phone, but soon after buying it, the front screen cracked. This made it so I was unable to read text messages without opening it first, or worse, I couldn't see who was calling before answering the phone. I had to pick up the call prior to knowing who was on the line, similar to how we used to answer landlines.

As we headed into LA, we were at the song Chloe was anxiously awaiting. Once it started playing, my phone lit up and vibrated, so she turned down the music for me to answer it. I flipped it open. It was just a text, not a call. It was from Zach: *Landed. I'll head to Southwest for pickup.*

We predicted exactly what he would be wearing: basketball shorts, Nike shoes, and a white T-shirt underneath a hooded sweatshirt. He was tall and lanky, so most clothes looked baggy on him. Then my phone lit up again, so she turned down her song with a sigh; his text let us know he would be at terminal 1.

As we pulled up, the 6'3" guy stuck out like a sore thumb. He got in the car and we sped off. Chloe quickly told him how he interrupted her song, so now he had to be quiet and listen to it.

As Chloe started it over for the third time, she turned the volume back up; we only got thirty seconds into the song and my phone lit up with a blank screen. We both looked at it, then each other. I turned down the music, slowly picked up the phone, and apologized to her, saying, "Chloe, I'm sorry, but I have to pick it up because I can't see who it is!"

Irritated, Chloe rolled her eyes.

"Hello?" I said, answering the phone.

Through my phone and from the backseat we heard, "What's up?"

Chloe whirled around in the front seat and yelled at Zach, "I'm gonna kill you!"

Zach always had a way to make me smile. He kept things lighthearted and didn't take anything too seriously. This is likely why we got along so well and never had any fights. We would see each other and, if he wasn't dating anyone, act as though we were still a couple and had never been apart.

He spent the weekend at our house and met all my roommates. They all loved his personality and how sweet he was with me. They, too, thought we were meant for each other.

After our time together sped by, and before dropping him back off at the airport, we went down to the beach for sunset. We took our shoes off and walked together in the sand near where the waves would come ashore. He grabbed my hand as we walked. We eventually came to a stop where he whirled me around to look him in his eyes. He pulled my hair back, said he loved me, then kissed me for a prolonged amount of time. It felt never-ending. It felt like a scene from a Nicholas Sparks or Colleen Hoover novel. It felt right.

It always did with him.

The Final Lap

Less than a month away from graduating, I was gearing up to live in Newport Beach with an old friend from high school (the same girl I traveled to London and Paris with), and I would be starting my "big-girl" job. I had received an offer from a public accounting firm to work as an auditor in the fall.

Senior year continued to be wild. There were a lot of comical scenarios and tangled webs going on. After dancing with drama myself with the "Indiana Jones Hat Thief," I did my best to stay off the gossip radar.

In the middle of craziness, Chloe and I would look at each other and say, "It's going in the book" as a response to any climactic event we were part of. It started to happen so often that no words were exchanged; just a simple look would suffice. Chloe and I had plans to publish a book together as coauthors ever since the first night we met.

One evening, while playing cards at a friend's house, a song called "The Best Is Yet to Come" came on the radio. Chloe and I looked at each other with wide-eyed grins and said in unison, "That's it! That's the title of our book!"

Next was graduation, and I was selected to give the student commencement speech. With no previous experience of speaking in front of a lot of people, I was told there would be around ten thousand in attendance. *Great*, I thought.

I anxiously called Lucas to tell him the news. Without missing a beat, he said, "I'm coming down."

Aside from Lauren and Erika, he was the best at staying in touch with me. He knew everyone from back home, and each time he would visit, he would meet my latest batch of roommates.

Lucas knew everyone in my life, and everyone in my life knew Lucas. He was personable and fun, and all my friends would ask when he was going to come visit next. He had that effect on people. He improved the mood of the room just by being in it. When he opened his mouth, he had an incredibly fun-loving and quirky personality that was hard not to love.

The last few days before graduation were jam-packed, and to top it off, I would be a bridesmaid in my friend's wedding the evening of graduation. I was busy getting hours in at work, finishing papers, calming my nerves for my upcoming speech, studying for finals, and getting my life in order. I was so busy with my to-do list that I wasn't even digesting what was about to happen—I would be done with college and discovering life in the real world.

My speech was titled "Living Your Purpose." It went better than expected with all my classmates, teachers, friends, family, and other spectators including Lucas in the audience. I talked about using whatever your major was in college, pairing it with your individual talents, and sharing those gifts by being a shining light to others. While I felt as if I was a complete advocate for this theme, I still wasn't entirely sure yet how my life would play out. It's funny how I could write and rehearse the perfect words to say, yet that didn't equate that I had *my* life and *my* purpose all figured out.

For so long, I didn't know where I belonged. When people would ask me where I was from, my answer felt convoluted and confusing. I knew God would use me in life; I knew that He uses all of us if we lean into His will. Yet I was still unsure what it was He wanted for me or how he was going to utilize me for His purpose.

Back Home

I continued to fly home multiple times each year, and the Tinky Winkies would come down every so often to visit. We would pick up where we left off—the jokes, the late-night sporadic milkshake or Blizzard, our constant discussions of boys, and our unfailing love for each other. We were the type of friends that even if life got busy and we went months without talking, once we were together, it was as though no time had passed.

At this point, we had graduated college, and life took each of us in separate directions. Even though some of us had boyfriends and other friends from college or work, the original six remained the same. I always knew, without a doubt, the bond we had was something a lot of people dream of having. They will always feel like home to me.

We had a weekend together the summer after my senior year and decided to have a night out in Bellingham to get away from the small-town bonfire that seemed as though everyone was attending. After an evening of dancing and seeing old friends, I rode back to Lauren's house toward our small town around 2:30 a.m.

On the drive home, Lauren got in a fight with her boyfriend, who happened to be at the bonfire. She hung up and peevishly asked if we could swing by.

When we pulled up, there were still a lot of cars there, even at this time in the morning. Walking down to the river, we passed a stumbling individual who exclaimed, "Heidi, I haven't seen you in years!" This indicated we were headed in the right direction.

As we approached the bonfire, I spotted Lauren's boyfriend with his friends. We walked right up and asked how their night was. Suddenly, I heard someone from behind me say, "No way!"

I slowly turned around. To my surprise, it was Zach. Still at the bonfire. Homeboy didn't even party. He gave me a huge hug and started hanging all over me. Immediately, I said, "All right, I'm driving you home."

I told Lauren that I would be taking him home since his house was conveniently across the street from hers. Thank goodness the first car my dad taught me to drive was a stick shift. Getting Zach's old Toyota truck out of the riverbank and over the dune took me a few tries, but then we were on our way.

As I pulled his truck up next to his house, I had flashbacks of when we were together. Images of us holding each other in high school flooded my mind and took me back to when things had been perfect between us and when there were only a few miles of separation.

I turned off his truck, smiled at him, and said, "You're welcome."

"Thanks for taking me home!" he replied instantly.

"Of course," I said.

He leaned over and kissed me softly.

I pulled back, stepped out of the truck, and closed the door behind me. I walked over to the passenger's side as he was getting out. He closed his door and, without hesitation, locked his arms around me and held me close.

After a few moments hugging, I uttered, "Okay, Zach. Have a good night."

"Will you please come tuck me in?"

"You're a big kid," I replied. "You can do it yourself."

"But I don't know where my room is."

I gave him a look.

"I'm being honest," he said. "After I left for college, my parents switched my room with my brother's."

"I can't."

"Why not?"

"I'm not falling for this."

"Heidi, please. You know I love you."

Irritated, I turned away toward Lauren's house just across the street. "Zach, I—"

Right then, he scooped me up and took my breath away. He held me close and kissed my lips as he walked into the house.

Although my entire body had been tense, I exhaled a sigh of relief. I wanted this ongoing saga to be over and for us to finally be together again. I wanted, more than anything, for life to revert back to the time when our relationship wasn't so complicated.

9

Adulting

Before my big-girl job started, I had an endless summer. I was determined to live carefree up until the very last day before the real world officially began. There wasn't a shortage of fun or events between a trip to Florida with Chloe's family, invitations to twelve weddings, a serendipitous visit from my North Carolina friend, and a weekend in Chicago with a road trip back to SoCal for me to borrow my sister's car while she was in Peru.

Once I arrived home and moved to Newport Beach, Lauren and Lucas were at my front doorstep for a visit. Living ninety-six steps to the sand, I spent a weekend with them and also enjoyed a full month of beach days before I had to report to the office.

My first three days at my new job consisted of training, admin, and logistics information. We booked flights through the company's account to Chicago to attend a week-long training the following week.

In my office, there were five of us who started together: three graduated from USC, one from Cal Poly San Luis Obispo, and then there was me, from a small private "no-name" university. Immediately, I felt inadequate. It also didn't help that I was the only girl there. One of the guys in my start group was tall, dark, and handsome, but I tried not to let it cloud my thinking.

I arrived in Chicago that next week and was met with a personal chauffeured car that took me to the training center. Once I arrived, I checked into my room, where they handed me the itinerary for the week. Our training would run from 8 a.m. to 5 p.m. for the next five days.

When the morning came, I went to get some food from the buffet breakfast. The dining hall was packed with professionals with their black work backpacks or side satchels. I was in black pants, a short-sleeved button-down top from Express, and awkwardly stood six feet tall in heels. After I ate with a few of the other new hires from my office, I made my way over to my designated room for training that day.

All cell service was blocked in the training rooms as well as internet and messaging on the computers, so there was nothing for us to do except listen to lectures for forty hours that week. We were trained on the different methods for testing. The testing is to ensure the validity of the financial statements for our clients. For many companies, their fiscal year end coincides with the end of the calendar year, so auditors will work what is called a "busy season," which typically consists of working a *lot* of hours from January through March to review the financial data of the prior year.

This new-hire training was for the first-time audit associates from all over the country. We were randomly placed in groups, and in my classroom, there were around twenty-five people. I quickly observed that I was likely the only one in the room who didn't previously intern, had passed absolutely zero sections of the CPA exam, and didn't have a master's degree. By the end of day one, I was crying on the floor of my tiny hotel room. I texted Chloe that evening in tears, saying, *I think I chose the wrong major.*

Once I was back working in the office, there were some managers and senior-level staff that were let go. One of them had been my hiring manager just a few months ago. Soon after, coworkers who had been hired with me at the same time in the Los Angeles office were laid off after just weeks on the job. I started to feel like I was the weakest link in my group at the office and that I would be the next to go.

My stress was at an all-time high one evening as I rushed out of the office to make it to yoga. This opportunity was a rarity after long hours of work paired with my commute to clients more than an hour away.

I arrived at the studio not even three minutes before class started. The studio was strict with late arrivals. I kicked off my heels and stepped into the hot yoga room packed with the 6:30 p.m. corporate-worker wave who were likely also retreating from the stress of their day. I barely found an open area to lay down my mat. It felt as if there was one tiny sliver of a spot left, just for me.

I tiptoed out as to not disturb anyone and rushed back to the ladies' room to put on long pants and a tank top. At this point, I was too self-conscious of my body to wear anything less, even though it is encouraged in the heat. I rushed back as the teacher was opening the door for me. I gestured a "thank you," and stepped into the hot room.

The teacher turned on the lights, welcomed us to class, and assisted with adjusting yoga mats to allow everyone a bit more space to be able to see themselves in the front mirror. She invited us to stand to begin our practice with *Pranayama* breathing. As we stood, she started her instructions with: "Leave your stress, worries, and day outside the door. Choose to let those things go. Begin by concentrating on your breath . . ."

I was annoyed. *This lady has no idea what kind of day I've had,* I thought. *How could I leave my stress? How could I think about anything else? I'm going to get fired from my job!*

And just like that, I was lying in my sweat in the final *savasana*. It was as if an alchemy event occurred and I had been transformed. Being stretched far too thin from working my corporate job under the constant worry that I would be fired, I entered the room unwilling to let go of my day weighed down by stress . . . and I left the room weightless.

The Shift

There I was, sitting in the cold and tiny audit room, starting on my first "cycle" (or category) for testing on my client. I was working on the cash section and stared blankly at a bank reconciliation—a worksheet used to balance bank statements to the clients' records. I flipped back and forth between the current and prior year to determine how to start testing and documenting in the workpaper. Although it likely appeared I was working hard, I was hardly working at all as my mind would wander and I would think about hypothetical things (like how I couldn't help but compare this Excel file to my own life).

My outer world had appeared this dream to others—I had relocated to Southern California, lived at the beach, received a well-paying offer at a prestigious firm straight out of college, yet, simultaneously, my inner world was discontent and disconnected. It felt confusing. The outcomes didn't mesh because what appeared to be living in happiness left me feeling empty inside. My inner and outer worlds didn't equate. They were unreconciled. *I* was unreconciled.

In an audit, when the amounts in the accounts don't match or pan out, this indicates there's been an accounting error. If the discrepancy is large enough, it is called a misstatement, and can even be big enough to be classified as a material misstatement which demands for more testing and more explanation as to why the clients' documents didn't equate to the numbers they were reporting. I knew, deep in my heart, if I carried on living this way, working at this job, playing the part that I was happy, my life, too, would be materially misstated.

For now, my motto was to work hard and play hard. While I knew I wasn't working at my forever job, I continued to doggy paddle in responsibilities, staying up to date on training, generally accepted accounting principles (GAAP), and juggling clients, barely keeping my head above water.

I came up for air from my first busy season, and that was when I took my trip to Peru to visit my middle sister. But three days before my plane took off, Lucas was in a terrible motorcycle accident.

Lauren was prompt at keeping me up to date on the status of his condition. He had injured his leg and ribs and had a broken arm. Right after the accident, I received a photo via text of him lying on the ground in his helmet, blood dripping down his pant leg, and something lying next to him in the gravel. It turned out to be two inches of his femur bone, which was completely outside of his body beside him. When I would follow up with Lauren every other day to ask how he was doing, she was always quick to respond with the same answer: "He's going to be fine, Heidi."

I wondered if she knew something that I didn't and thought that I might freak out if I actually knew the truth.

I couldn't stop thinking about him. Feelings of helplessness lingered while I traveled around South America. I prayed he would be okay. What would I do without him?

Our trip started in Lima, and we made our way to Huaycan, where my middle sister was volunteering. She got connected with a friend who started a nonprofit school to teach English to the young children in the town.

While Lima reminded me of big cities in Spain, Huaycan was unlike anything I had ever seen before. I couldn't believe how people lived in those conditions. We brought clothes and school supplies from the States to give to the kids and stayed there for a few nights to meet my sister's new friends and watch her teach the children who all loved her dearly. I was bewildered how happy they were with so little. After this important stop, we continued on our tour of the rest of Peru, visited Machu Picchu, and ended our trip in Rio de Janeiro.

When we booked our tickets, the Machu Picchu attraction was closed. They had suffered terrible floods there, and it wasn't safe to visit the natural wonder. This made our plane tickets significantly cheaper since it is usually one of the biggest draws for tourists to travel to Peru. It didn't faze me, as our purpose for going was to visit my sister in her new environment.

However, just a couple weeks prior to takeoff, we learned Machu Picchu had reopened. My sister adjusted the itinerary, and we visited one of the Seven Wonders of the World! It was meant to be.

Machu Picchu was the confirmation I needed at that time. I felt reassured that I was on the right path. I knew I wanted out of the career I was in, I knew I wanted to volunteer and do something to start making a difference, and I knew I needed to start letting go of the things in my life that brought me down, because, in reality, there was so much good in my life.

While in Cuzco, the closest city to Machu Picchu, we visited one of the villages that was swept away in the floods. We brought food, blankets, and basic household items for the people who lived there.

The neediness and devastation left a mark on my heart. These people had lost their homes and didn't even know if they were going to sleep warmly at night or eat the next day.

Meanwhile, back home, I was stressed about work, passing the CPA exam, and Lucas's condition. And I continued to wonder when Zach and I would finally live happily ever after.

It became very apparent that my stresses were temporary . . . that I had the power to change my environment, and if I wanted to switch careers, nobody was stopping me. In my heart, I knew that if Zach and I were meant to be together, we would work out; Lucas's condition kept improving, and I continued to pray that he would survive and be able to walk again.

Seeing my sister volunteer in a third-world country created a spark in me. *That's living life*, I thought. She was visibly making a difference for the better in the lives of people who needed it most.

I wanted something in my life that brought more fulfillment, but I wasn't sure what that was for me just yet. I felt bad that I hadn't made the jump to live somewhere like Peru to make a difference in the world, yet I wondered, *How can I make a difference in the world when I'm not even making a difference in my own community*? Sure, my job is important, but I wanted to make an impact outside of auditing financial statements or my interactions in the office.

This prompted me to write a bucket list with big goals:

Bucket List

1. Complete the role as a senior on my public company audit
2. Become yoga certified
3. Volunteer at a nonprofit in Orange County and at church
4. Run a marathon
5. Visit Big Sur, Banff, Bora Bora, and Bali
6. See Coldplay in concert
7. Marry the love of my life and travel to Europe together
8. Save $20,000
9. Become a mom
10. Write my book

After I returned home and grinded through four days of work, I hopped on a flight for a quick trip to visit Lucas after his accident. Most of my time there was spent talking with him as he sat in a hospital bed at his parents' house. It was so great to see him but so unusual to see him like that.

But he is okay!

That's what mattered.

Like a Ton of Bricks

Once returning back to California, I was ready to start making strides to change my reality. While working with an out-of-town client in Palm Springs, and after a very long day, my coworker and I returned to our hotel with the final moments of a UV index where you could still get a tan. We saw a girl at the pool with sunglasses on, relaxing in the sunshine, obviously enjoying her stay in the desert more than we were. My coworker turned to me and confessed, "I wish I had her life. She doesn't even know what an audit is."

My job continued to stress me out. There was a weekend where I lost twelve pounds in less than a three-day span. I felt sharp pain in my lower abdomen and couldn't eat.

After multiple doctor appointments and tests later, they all came back with the same conclusion: you're healthy. While that may sound like a relief to most, which it certainly was, it didn't explain my rapid weight loss or excruciating pain. The only thing that made sense was it was likely due to the stress I was holding in my body.

It was then that I signed up to be a "Big" (a big sister) through the Big Brothers Big Sisters program. It was a long process.

They asked me to fill out pages of background questions paired with providing my fingerprints. After months of waiting, I was matched with a fourteen-year-old girl. I felt nervous and wondered, *What if she doesn't like hanging out with me? What if we don't get along?*

Her profile said she loved music, so I thought maybe we could jive with that, and then I read her name: Erika . . . just like one of my closest friends from back home. I took it as a sign and chose not to worry about it.

I started meeting up with my "Little" (my little sister) a couple times a month. We would go to the beach, get ice cream, grab dinner—simple things. She would talk to me about school and the dilemmas that arose between her and her friends. She always sounded like the voice of reason in her friend group, and I was proud of her. Although she was so young, she was wise beyond her years.

After many hangouts, there was an afternoon we planned to meet up. I was stressed out and couldn't shake it. I remained under increasing pressure to study and pass the CPA exams, had a lot on my plate at work, *and* I was still single.

On my way to pick her up, I thought, *I don't have time for this! Why am I meeting up with her? Why did I sign up for this?*

Her mom texted to meet up at the park around the corner from the library, our usual pickup location. Once I arrived, my Little jumped in my car, and we waved goodbye to her mom. I put on an exhilarated expression, added "Hi!!" and we shared a hug. As I was about to pull away, I asked, "Where does your mom want us to meet later?"

"Oh, you can meet back here at the park."

"The park . . ." I slowly responded, "but it will be really late."

"Yeah, that's fine. We've been sleeping here. Well, not here, but in the car for the last two weeks."

My heart catapulted into the pit of my stomach. With her words, it felt like everything became clear. Here I was "stressed to the max" about things that didn't matter. Meanwhile, for the last two weeks, my little sister was sleeping in a car.

A week or so later, I was sitting at work. There were two partners with us at my public client chatting about nonwork-related topics. One had two young girls, maybe ages eight and ten, and the other had a two-year-old daughter. They were discussing their children's bank accounts and how they were saving money for them. Yet the way they talked about it, they sounded disconnected. They, too, were complaining about first world problems: the price of raising children and how much college and their future weddings would cost them.

My heart strings tightened, and all I could think about was my little sister sleeping in a car. *How were they so consumed in the box they call their life? Don't they know how great they have it?* I know they're just trying to provide for their families, but there were little kids out there with nothing to their name, not even a bed.

The Beginning

The remainder of that summer was full of weddings, trips to the river and San Diego, and many escapades with Chloe. My beach rental in Newport was up, so Chloe, her friend Ella, and I talked about finding a place together. Ella didn't typically start drama, but drama seemed to follow her (as well as funny encounters). She was a dependable friend; everyone enjoyed her company, and she was always down for a fun night, especially if it included swimming in fountains.

One evening, we met up with an old friend from college who was out with one of his high school friends in Costa Mesa. They were both from the area. Chloe and I had plans to move out, and so did they.

"Let's all live together!" Chloe shrieked.

I wasn't sold on the idea. But finding a house for five people (which would also include Ella) and splitting it would be much more cost effective. I knew my parents wouldn't approve of me living with boys, but as the conversation continued with lots of jokes and laughs, it was obvious it would be a fun mix. One of their other friends we met that evening was fully supportive and said that he wouldn't pay rent but would happily crash on our couch.

Chloe and I got in the car to head home after our fun evening. I got in the driver's seat and was staring at Chloe as she closed her door, put her seatbelt on, and pulled her phone out. She was completely unaware of my eyes on her. After almost a minute passed, she looked at me.

"What?" she asked, startled.

"You like him," I said.

"Who?" she asked.

"The couch guy," I said.

"How do you know?!" she asked, giggling.

"Because I know your type. He's it."

The next week, Ella came out with us to meet the two boys who would presumably be our new roommates. She loved them, and our fate was sealed. We all shook on it, took shots to celebrate, and would commence our search for a house big enough for five people.

It was the beginning of our little family.

Part 3

*There is no telling how many miles
you will have to run while chasing a dream.*

—Unknown

10

Someone Like You

My pace began to increase. I was no longer concentrating on my steps and was taking huge strides rapidly. My breath had to catch up to the speed my body was moving. I looked down at my watch: I made it.

I hit my goal pace under eight minutes a mile for 6.22 miles. I started to slow down and came to a complete halt while gasping for breath. I hunched over and placed my hands on my knees as the sweat from my brow dripped onto my bright pink Nikes.

I started running regularly to build up my endurance for a marathon. While a 10k was our annual trot on Thanksgiving, I had gotten a bit out of shape since the previous year and had a ways to go to build my stamina to eventually run an additional twenty miles.

Once I gained my composure, I started to walk with my hands on my hips for the last bit of the path next to the rushing river. The foliage was stunning, with different shades of vivid red and orange hues. There was a light chill in the air since it was late September in the Midwest, and it was time for me to go in, shower, and report for dinner.

I was back in the suburb of Chicago for my second year of work-related training. But this time, I was here with a completely different attitude. After day one of training, I had confidence I could easily blow through the modules and tests the remainder of the week with ease.

In my first year of auditing, my seniors exposed me to all aspects of the job. So by the time I attended my second year of training, and after working sixty- to seventy-hour work weeks during the busy season, I learned a lot and improved my skills in a little under one year. It's a testament to discipline. When you are thrown into the deep end and forced to stay afloat, you are bound to learn exponentially, or you sink and could get fired.

The few days before my week-long training, I enjoyed the weekend with my sister in the city, since she had recently returned from Peru. One of her friends rented a party trolley for barhopping that weekend, and I was invited to join in on the fun.

We stopped at a bar where there was a high school reunion. My sister and I each grabbed a drink and a name tag that read something like Katie or Hannah. A group of people walked up to us and struck up a conversation about how different we looked; after engaging in about a five-minute chat with them, we bolted when their heads were turned. My sister and I sped out of the bar laughing and headed back to the trolley. As we climbed the steps, we found everyone else was already back on the trolley, cheering for us, and all wearing name tags. We hadn't been the only ones. Yet these were no longer names from the high school reunion: someone had snagged a stack of blank tags and was writing names like The President, Paul Bunyan, Ludacris, or Katy Perry. That late night turned early morning held incessant laughter and dancing.

It felt like there was a shift in my life where I was leaning into this spark I got from exhilarating adventures. These moments felt hard to put into words. They were so magical, coincidental, and hilarious that I continued having instances I felt were meant for a movie with a great storyline. That same month, Chloe and I randomly ran into the "Indiana Jones Hat Thief" at a Goo Goo Dolls concert in LA. He made a point to flag us down, and we carried on an awkward conversation. I'm not sure what the stars were thinking that day, aligning for us to have that moment, but maybe it was to keep me on my toes and remind me just how far I had come.

After these two unanticipated events, I attended one of Zach's college football games. That saga seemed to continue. He was playing for a school in Northern California, and they happened to be playing at a local spot close to me. He was busy as a collegiate athlete, and I was busy with work and inserting fun into my schedule every chance I could. I was happy to see him and, as always, left wondering when and how we were going to end up back together again. After the game, we hugged before he retreated to the locker room for a shower and dinner with his coaches and teammates. While walking back to my car to leave, my phone buzzed with an incoming text.

Thank you so much for coming, it read.

Of course, I quickly replied.

You know I love you, he responded.

Oriole Drive

After a lot of searching, the five of us soon-to-be roommates found the ideal spot in Costa Mesa. The weekend after moving in, we had our first official party. Chloe and I went to grab a drink, and as we were patiently waiting our turn, a guy at the party asked, "So, do you live around here?"

We looked at each other, then back at him, and replied in unison, "Yeah. Upstairs."

The kitchen was so big that for weeks at a time we kept a beer pong table in the middle, and there was still plenty of additional space in the room. It would be no surprise to find something inappropriately scripted on the fridge with magnetic letters. I felt as though I was constantly laughing, living with these clowns. The living situation filled my need for fun and adventure during my grueling job.

Social events were always waiting for me inside our home. Whether we were playing video games, having Bieber dance-offs, chatting at 2 a.m. with our guy roommate dancing around in my fedora, or grabbing some Yogurtland after speeding through the streets of Costa Mesa blasting Miley Cyrus with the windows down and singing at the top of our lungs; there was always something happening. Not only did fun follow us, but it was brought along wherever we would go.

While drowning in busy season, our entertaining house is what kept me going, and I would squeeze in yoga classes when I could to help bring my stress level down. I made a point not to let my job consume me: I would reassure myself that I was making good money and would stay at my firm until I paid off school, then I would jump ship once I determined what career I wanted to pursue next.

I arrived home late one night from work, and the roomies were all fast asleep. I felt sorry for myself working such long hours, and the FOMO was undeniable. The house was dark, so I flicked on the light in the kitchen. I noticed the colorful letters on the fridge were arranged to read "I love this Fam Bam." I smiled. I knew the end of my long hours of busy season were in sight; I just had to make it through some more busy workweeks.

I resurfaced from busy season to attend a Lakers game. It was my first time seeing Kobe Bryant play in real life. His swagger emanated throughout the entire building. Even though our seats were high up in the Staples Center, his dominance down on the floor was palpable. Kobe hit three 3-pointers in a twenty-second span. I had never seen such an impressive athlete before. Sure, he was cocky, but the man was a legend.

Only a few minutes into the game, my friend and I got up from our section for a quick restroom break and ran into Magic Johnson. I was sure glad I had to use the bathroom right at that moment! Once we returned to our seats, I felt my phone buzz. I looked down at my Blackberry. It was Zach. I rolled my eyes. Typical.

His text was initiating small talk, but I offered only short responses in return as I was trying to watch the game. I wasn't invested in the conversation, but I could tell he *was*. He started talking about this girl at college; I guess they were dating. I continued not to take it seriously because he told me he loved me just a few months ago, and here he was again, still talking to me.

My phone buzzed over and over, reminding me that I hadn't looked at the message. I looked down and read his text: *She's pregnant.*

Harsh Reality

A few weeks later, I was completing the quarterly review for my public client. Sitting in our small audit room discussing an issue with my senior, he gave me his reply to a controversial topic and how I needed to document the accounting in my workpapers. His eyes were locked on me after a long pause and my lack of response to his extremely detailed and long-winded answer. He irritably prompted me with the question, "Are you happy?"

I felt a shudder race through my body.

I thought to myself, *Happy, as in, am I satisfied with his response? Happy, as in, do I need anything further? Happy, as in, am I happy in life?* But at the initial impact of his question, my throat tightened up, my eyes began to water, and my heart sank. While I was asked a seemingly simple question, I withheld the depth of my actual answer. I knew I wasn't happy; how could I be when the presumed love of my life was going to be a dad? To cover up my uncontrollable emotions, I blurted out a short, unconvincing laugh, broke eye contact, and replied, "Ha. Yeah, I'm happy with your answer. Thank you."

I didn't want to start crying in the middle of the audit room. I didn't know what it would take for the news to finally hit me, and I didn't *want* it to hit. Sure, I wasn't going to end up with the love of my life and my heart was crushed, but even more so, I knew I wasn't happy. There was no chance of us ever being together again, and he would no longer exist in my life.

Last time we talked, Zach said he loved me and that every girl he dated wasn't right. Then, fast-forwarding to our most recent text conversation, he told me this girl was pregnant. He didn't tell me when she was due, and I didn't ask. It didn't matter. Once I learned the news, that was it. I figured she would have her baby before the end of the year, so I went to bed crying most nights with no plans to speak to him ever again.

Swim

The next month, all five of the roomies were at home on a Sunday night, which was a rarity for us all. Between work, our social lives, and conflicting schedules, not a lot of weekends were spent together at home. We were hanging out and laughing uncontrollably about a story one of the guys was telling when my phone buzzed. I was curious to see who it was since we were all together and had no plans for other friends to join us that evening.

I looked down at my Blackberry; there was solely an attachment of a JPEG, which seemed odd. I figured it was spam but was curious and clicked on it anyway. When it loaded, I saw a photo of a baby wearing a pink hat, wrapped in a standard hospital blanket. My heart sank. While I knew this moment was inevitable, it was already here.

I congratulated him on his daughter.

I showed Chloe the photo. Her eyes got huge. She blurted, "Holy—Heidi, I'm *so* sorry." I, too, was in disbelief.

"Of course he had a girl," she stated.

"Why does that matter?" one of my guy roommates chimed in.

"Because it just means he's going to be that much more attached. Girls have a way of wrapping their daddy around their finger . . ."

As she continued explaining, I zoned out. Regardless, the invisible string I thought had kept us connected for so many years was finally cut. Although I had been content at home with my roommates, my emotions took a major turn, and I knew I couldn't sit with them and pretend I wasn't affected by the news. I had to leave, but I had nowhere to go. I made the excuse that I would head into the office to study for my CPA exam, which loomed over my head, so I packed up my laptop and workbook and was out the front door.

I got in my car, started the engine, and was instantly on autopilot. I took my normal route, made all the same turns, parked in a familiar spot, and was soon walking up to my building, only eight minutes from our house.

The elevator dinged as I stepped out and made my way to the cubicles I would often reserve if I wasn't working on a client and had a free day in the office. The audit-team cubicles sat across from the partners' offices, which had the best views overlooking Orange County. There wasn't another person in the office this late on a Sunday night.

I sat down and booted up my laptop. I sharpened a few pencils, then started to read. I read for a few minutes about GAAP, but I soon realized I was not *really* reading. I was turning the pages but digesting nothing. Breathing and living life but not feeling anything.

For the last three weeks, I had been going through the motions. I was desensitized. I was in denial. I was depressed.

After a few minutes, it hit me like a tidal wave. Tears continuously rolled down my cheeks. I was sobbing so hard, I had no idea what I would say if someone walked in at that moment. But I didn't care. My heart was shattered.

I never wrapped my brain around us not being together because I believed everything he said. Even though I moved away and he dated other girls, it always felt like he was trying to get back to me or that he wanted to be with me instead. But, for all I know, they were just words to keep me in his back pocket. I didn't truly consider the possibility of ending up with anyone other than him. And that is why the sting was so strong. I had to grieve someone who didn't die, yet he could no longer exist in my life.

It became clear to me that I avoid things. I avoid people if they make me mad, I avoid feelings if they make me sad, and I avoid thoughts if they make me scared. For so long, I had tried to be strong during all the changes in my life. After I moved in high school, transferred colleges, worked at different jobs, and had to find new friends again and again based on location, I wanted to control *something*. I wanted to keep something in my life constant and not be affected by the perpetual adjustments. It was easier to look pathetic and hold onto something over a thousand miles away rather than jump into a new relationship I was not emotionally ready for.

It didn't feel random that Adele's "Someone Like You" came out a few months prior to me learning the new information that Zach was having a baby. That song gave me the words I didn't know I felt, which was what I needed to get through every day.

I was accustomed to writing as a way for me to express my thoughts or feelings, but I didn't write anything down for a long time. I had a hard time accepting the turn of events and knew if I wrote how I felt on paper, it would confirm my reality. I was still in the avoidance stage, and if I jotted down what happened, it would reiterate that the photo of a little baby created a finality in my life. Our relationship felt incomplete. There was never anything further said. There was never even a goodbye.

I knew that sixteen-year-old me would always love him. But that was long ago. Now our story was over.

Turn for the Better

That same week, the doorbell rang, and a loud knock quickly followed. The roomies had been discussing that *someone* who lived around the corner may be taking *someone* on a date. The funny thing was the couch guy usually didn't knock or ring the doorbell; he would just walk right in.

But this was official business.

After catching wind of this highly anticipated event, one of the guy roomies and I army crawled to peek through the white 1980s-style railing. We peered into the foyer downstairs, where we had a direct view of what was unfolding.

Within seconds, Chloe opened the door. There stood the "couch surfer" on the porch, holding flowers. He handed them to her, and with a kiss on the cheek, they were on the other side of that big blue door, off to their first date. Once the door closed behind them, my roomie turned to me with wide eyes and announced, "Shit just got real!"

It was official. Our couch surfer was dating Chloe.

One of the reasons Chloe and I became friends was our shared desire to write a book. We both were holding onto our first love and had other synchronicities and similarities in our lives. We had flings at the exact same time and would navigate our relationships together. When events happened to each of us simultaneously, it encouraged us to write a book of our shared and coincident lives. It wasn't until now, when I completely lost my first love and Chloe found a new love, that the previous synchronicity shifted.

I was so grateful that I lived with these hooligans at the same time that my love life officially died. There was never a dull moment and always a story to share each day. We could have had our own reality TV show. Like the night Ella came home crying with both of our guy roommates because she saw her ex-boyfriend out at a bar and slapped him. Or the time cops showed up to the house after receiving a call about a loud party, and one of the boys answered the knock at the door while in the middle of doing laundry at home by himself.

It felt impossible to stay sad in a house of people who kept me laughing. One of the boys choreographed a dance to "Fork in the Garbage Disposal," while the other one talked crap on all the trendy stuff Chloe attempted. We had a unison house response of "You won't" as a motivating push to get another roommate to act outside of their comfort zone. There was always someone to chat with regarding daily drama, and my favorite nights included walks to the bluffs which provided a view of the city lights below the hills and nothing but stars above. I enjoyed nightly pillow talks with Chloe since we shared the master bedroom, which was large enough to effortlessly fit two queen beds. There were no secrets in the house since we told each other everything. The entertainment value was at max capacity, and it was nonstop. It kept me from dwelling on the state of my broken heart.

My life was busy like never before. I had confirmations for flights or hotels filling up my email. I felt a panic every time I left for the airport to double- or triple-check which airport I was flying out of.

Trips and events filled every weekend, even doubling up some weekends, but I needed the distraction. That summer, I ended up traveling to ten states. My life was too eventful for me to sit with my feelings. It was one of the busiest and most full years of my life. My schedule masked any void I felt inside as I was consumed with work and my social life. It felt like too much yet not enough. It didn't matter what was happening or going on for me at that time. No weeklong trip to Mexico, free trip to Vegas, or countless trips to see the Tinky Winkies (even including two of their weddings) could ease my anguish. And in the middle of my heartache, I had four roomies who kept my spirits at an all-time high. I knew there was a bright side somewhere.

Prior to take-off from my last trip late that fall, I texted my roommate a question about the house and let him know when I would be arriving back home. He responded, *Yeah, I'll be around. I've had a lot of time to try on your thongs with you gone.* These boy roommates were the big brothers I always wanted but never had . . . until now.

11

Friends

Ever since moving to SoCal, I had been working my way to get back "home" to Washington. That next March, I was scheduled to work two weeks on a subsidiary for a client in Seattle.

I got to see friends and family who lived in the area. Lauren and I spent the most time together to reconvene, which was always needed. She's been my person who understands my heart without any words spoken. We view life the same way, and she is often my sounding board when I'm wavering on a question or decision. Even as time passed and the miles between us never seemed to dissipate, we were always the closest.

All the Tinky Winkies went to Seattle for a rendezvous, making my time spent there extra special, and it even snowed, adding just a touch of peace and magic to my visit. In the midst of all those feel-good times, it was this trip that I had some realizations.

First, I visited a Bikram yoga studio. I'm not typically one to practice yoga while traveling, but I was staying with my friend who was scheduled to work late one night at the hospital, so I decided to go check out the local studio. The teacher and vibe of the location was interesting and different from my studios back in California.

When I entered the yoga space, there were only two other students and me in the class. Once the teacher stepped foot in the room and started the same Bikram instructions, it was hard not to notice her eclectic mix of patterns since her top clashed with her pants. She wore thick glasses that fogged up in the hot and humid space. It was while taking this class that I told myself, *If she can be a yoga teacher, I can be a yoga teacher.*

Toward the tail end of my trip, I had another aha moment. My weeks spent there felt like déjà vu mixed with coincidence and confusion. Here I was, working in Seattle for my accounting firm, and this moment, exactly like it was, could have been my life. But if that had been the case, my life would only be here: this place and these friends. All those people from my new high school, club volleyball, my first college, my second college, studying abroad, my coworkers, my Costa Mesa roommates—none of them would have had any part in my life. The places I went, the relationships I made, the hard times I got through—wouldn't have happened.

It reminded me of the movie *It's a Wonderful Life*, where George Bailey is shown what his life would have looked like without him. And I told myself that if this was still the life I wanted, for Washington to be my home once again, I could move back. I could put in for a transfer, I could apply to work at another firm, I could relocate and move home.

But it was the first time I felt I didn't want to stay. I had inadvertently made California my new home. I loved my life there, as confusing as it was or as torn as it had once made me feel. Although moving back was something I had longed for since the moment I left, I was living such a full life, and I needed this trip to realize my life was unfolding exactly how it was meant to. And the reality was, it was better than I had imagined it would be.

The Frogs

Over a year had passed since learning Zach was a dad. His mom randomly messaged me on Facebook asking how I was doing and for my address. I had no inclination why she was reaching out, so I responded with the details and asked why she needed it.

Days later, I received a response: "A wedding invite, of course!"

There were two occasions scheduled: a ceremony in California and a reception in Washington. What were the odds that I was already scheduled to be out of the country for both? I would be working with a client in Canada, then we had our annual camping trip to Mexico, both occurring during each event. It made declining the request easy with no second-guessing whether or not I should attend.

I had been single for so long, but at this point in time, holding onto what was no longer mine wasn't in my best interest.

Remember the cute guy I mentioned from my start group that I chose *not* to focus on? The one who was tall, dark, and handsome? Well, we had worked together for almost two years, and there seemed to be sparks between us, or so I was told.

He and I had several picture-perfect moments. One time, I was walking to the office from the parking garage in a pencil skirt and heels. I am likely the most uncoordinated person to walk in high heels on the face of the planet. I had a box full of audit papers and supplies, so he jogged over to grab it from me and carry it into the office. It was literally a scene from a rom-com.

He had also been there to help us move into our house with my four other roommates. It was raining outside, but he offered to let me use his truck and helped me load large furniture in the rain. And we all know that nobody actually *wants* to help someone move.

Weeks later, we had him over for "family" dinner at the house where he met my crazy roommates. He fit right in comfortably and was cracking jokes. The roomies all let me know they approved of us dating, although I had been completely closed off to the idea until now.

He would invite me to go out with his friends, which I usually declined as I had enough of a social life already. But there was a time I agreed and attended a party at one of his friend's houses. He then left me at the party, so I fended for myself. It felt erratic. I thought, *Maybe we are just friends?*

After he left, I inadvertently hit it off with one of *his* best friends who kissed me, got my number, and texted me for two weeks straight, only to then completely ghost me thereafter. Although I waited it out, I never heard from him again.

Months later, I took matters into my own hands. Erika was in town for a visit, and I mustered up the courage to go to this guy's favorite bar he had been raving about that night we kissed.

As I showed the bouncer my ID and we stepped inside the Irish pub, I instantly saw him sitting at the bar. So, with nothing to lose, I walked right up to him as Erika went to use the restroom. His face lit up when I approached, and his warm smile was quickly followed by a hug. He bought me a drink and we started chatting. I skipped to the reason I had come and with confidence asked him point-blank:

"So why did you stop talking to me?"

Without hesitation, he answered, "Because my friend told me to."

How confusing. My coworker didn't want his friend to talk to me, but he also wasn't talking to me?

When I relayed the story to my roommates, they all jumped up and down and exclaimed "Heidi! Your coworker likes you! That's why he doesn't want his friend to talk to you!"

A week or so later, we had a party at our house, where my handsome coworker joined in with all the Costa Mesa crazies. It was obvious to everyone he was flirting with me. He would whisper in my ear and rub my back during a basic game of beer pong since we had paired off as a team. In between games, I went into the kitchen where my girl roommates were freaking out and, under their breath, saying, "Oh my gosh, Heidi! He's so into you!"

Before he left that evening, it was just the two of us saying goodbye as we sat in his truck before he headed home. Coldplay's "Yellow" was playing on the radio, one of my favorite songs, so I took it as confirmation that this must be my moment. I also had some liquid courage, so I went for it.

"There's something I've been meaning to tell you . . . I *like* you. I have for a while now," I said.

You know when silence feels like eternity? Yeah, me too. Okay, maybe it was only fifteen seconds. I expected a response, even a negative one, but I never expected zero response. After a long, awkward silence, I stepped out of the truck and went inside.

Coldplay, you let me down.

I continued to find myself at the end of each failed love story, often confusing and bizarre, with no one. Why did it have to be so challenging? Any seeming glimmer of hope of a love connection would crash and burn. This was yet another of my pathetic love debacles to add to my list:

1. Chloe and I met a cute guy at a Redbox in front of a gas station around the corner from our house. After chatting with him, he seemed totally normal, so we invited him over. Once there, he then carried on a one-sided twenty-minute conversation about mold.
2. I finally drew the line with a guy I went back and forth with for years when he unveiled his eighteenth tattoo. That's exactly when he confirmed he wanted to be with me.
3. There was a guy from college who leaned in for a kiss and after kissing me whispered, "I think I'm dating the wrong Heidi."
4. Then there was a boy from Newport who wrote me a multiple-page poem bound together in book form, complete with pictures and construction-paper cutouts he gifted me as a birthday present. He did this two years in a row!
5. Or the guy from Florida I connected with through a mutual friend, and we discovered we wanted the exact same name for our firstborn child.

One Sunday I attended church with my parents. I was at the peak of my frustration with habitually being single. While I believed in love, it started to feel as though love was meant for everybody but me. Between my stretches of traveling for work or helping out at Children's Church during the services, I would often miss the Sunday message. During this busy time of my life, however, it felt like when I was able to listen to the sermon, it was always exactly what I needed to hear.

The message was called "Finding the Love of Your Life." The part that stood out to me was the three points that must be met for a couple to work: spiritual unity, life-purpose compatibility, and both being emotionally healthy. The points made sense and sounded pretty straightforward. Yet no one at that point in my life had ticked all three boxes.

Self-Love

I didn't realize how much I needed to change. For a long time, my life had been in a state of flux—the school I attended, the place I called home, and the people I hung out with—yet it continued to be the same flawed me on the inside.

I dropped in at a Bikram studio around the corner from my house. The teacher, tall with dark hair and light eyes, spoke words that touched my heart. We were in standing bow pulling pose, one of the more challenging postures, and she honed in on noticing our thoughts and what we were telling ourselves when we were practicing in class. She explained, "If you tell yourself you're going to fall out of the posture, you will fall out. If you tell yourself you're awesome, you got this, keep kicking, then you might maintain your balance. What you say and what you believe becomes your reality. Notice what you tell yourself. *You* need to be your own biggest cheerleader. Nobody else is going to do it for you."

While this may seem obvious to some, I had never noticed it for myself before.

Back in high school, my basketball coach talked about positive thinking when it came to shooting free throws at basketball practice. It was a similar concept: you needed to visualize yourself making the shot before even shooting the ball. The process entailed concentrating on the hoop, setting your form, and following through on your shot, all with the confidence that the ball was going through the hoop. A free-throw is unlike any other shot you take in the game since it is the same distance to the hoop every single time and free of a defender. It's just you, the ball, the basket, and your mindset.

I realized I wasn't setting myself up for success. I had spoken negatively to myself most of my life. Just like this yoga teacher suggested, I started to become more aware of my thoughts. Not just during yoga class, but all the time.

Some people call this the "voice inside your head," while others refer to it as your ego. In my life, and especially during my yoga practice, my negative self-talk never seemed to take a break. From the moment I would set my mat down in the hot room and then sit and wait for class to begin, I would tell myself things like, "You're the biggest person in this room." Then, while in different postures, I would tell myself, "You're going to fall out of this posture" and "You're not good enough."

To change your thought process, first you must simply *notice* the thoughts. Then you need to take the correct steps to adjust what it is you are allowing yourself to think. For years, I was the meanest person to me, and I didn't even realize it. I learned you should talk to yourself like you were your own best friend.

Along the way, I learned that choosing your thoughts can be just like choosing what outfit you're going to wear for the day. If you select a top out of your closet, maybe you even try it on, but aren't too keen on the color or the way it fits or feels, you have the option and choice to simply put it back and grab something different. Just like choosing our thoughts: if you're ruminating over something in your head that serves you no purpose, simply put it out of your mind and choose to think about something else.

In Bikram yoga, you hold the postures for a set amount of time, then, once you release, there is either a moment of stillness (or even a *savasana*) where you're motionless; you're essentially sitting in your body's sensations and feelings before transitioning to the next pose. You don't have the option to run away or distract your mind with the next thing until it's time. Instead, you surrender to your thoughts and body's process of growth and healing.

I needed stillness in my life. My past required space for healing. I needed to start with my awareness and then actively change the narrative I would tell myself in my head every single day. Even though I exuded a happy, confident exterior, I was negative and consistently hard on myself. I had to let go of the fact that I was still single; instead, I needed to love *me* for the right person to come into my life and love me too.

The One Where We Say Goodbye

Changes were happening in and around me. We were nearing the end of the five-roommate era. Chloe decided to move back home, and Ella was pushing to find an apartment for just the two of us without the boys. I was sad we were "breaking up."

I've had a lot of amazing times in my life, but living in that house with those four other humans was inimitable. It felt like we lived our own version of the sitcom *Friends*. The daily shenanigans were matched with the genuine love, advice, and respect we gave each other. Most importantly, someone always had your back, no matter what guy was breaking your heart or whom you punched at a bar. While working crazy hours and traveling a lot, I always wanted to come home to their faces at night. We felt like a family, and, looking back, that's exactly what we were.

12

Feel Again

After the roommate exodus, Ella and I moved to the other side of the back bay in Newport Beach. The boys also moved to the same apartment complex one building over from us so we were still in proximity of one another.

It was different living with just Ella: our place stayed cleaner, our weeknights were low-key, and we had less parties. It allowed us to become much closer, and our friend circle started to change.

But at the end of summer, I hit a wall.

I've learned that I can hold on as long as there's an end in sight. I was trying to do the right things: volunteer teaching at Children's Church, serving as a big sister to my Little, improving my yoga practice paired with my mental health, and training for a marathon. I was trying to be the best version of myself. I was a guest at countless weddings, and I continued to attend them solo. But toward the end of that summer, I encountered an eventful week:

MONDAY—I drove to Walgreens to pick up photos I had ordered. It was pouring rain (of course it was, to add to the dramatization of my evening), and I hit every red light possible. Once I arrived at the store and hurried inside, the clerk couldn't find any pictures under my name. Puzzled, after more than five minutes of the lady searching while I browsed my emails to find the confirmation on my phone, I realized I ordered them at a *different* Walgreens on the other side of town.

Embarrassed, I apologized and stepped back into the rain without a coat and got in my car. I sat there, drenched, and started crying. My frustration from my efforts and life felt as though they were pounding down on me from the storm outside and in my head.

Why did true love seem to happen for everyone around me, except *me*? I was taught to pray, thank God for what you have, ask Him for what you need, and end the prayer with an amen. But, at this point, I had done that my whole life and things still seemed to remain the same. I was alone.

I pulled up to my parents' house. I parked and turned the engine off. My headlights stayed on with the incessant rain hitting my car. Then a white rabbit hopped across the street in front of me. It reminded me of the rabbit I saw on my road trip back in college when we were almost hit by a semi. Maybe this was His way of telling me it was in His hands and out of my own.

TUESDAY—I went on a date with the "perfect guy," and one of my coworkers tagged along; she had been eager to set the two of us up for months. I don't remember why she joined the date, but I was extremely grateful she was there.

Previously, while sitting in the audit room at work, she had gone on and on about how wonderful this guy was and how we would be a power couple. Well, a guy can be good-looking and theoretically a great catch based on an impressive resume, but our conversation over dinner was dry, quite like the champagne I held in my hand.

Somehow, we landed on the topic of the Dave Matthews Band, who I had seen in concert at the Gorge a few years back, and this was the *only* thing we had common ground on. His lack of personality made our conversation feel as though I was constantly reaching for any kind of commonality. Maybe I should have tried talking about mold.

WEDNESDAY—Ella and I were guest bartenders at Sharkeez in downtown Huntington Beach. Our friend was the manager, and he took us behind the bar to show us how to make drinks. I poured Jack into a cup followed by some Coca-Cola and he said, "Okay, great job pouring, but never, *ever* pour that much Jack into a cup ever again."

It was a wild and memorable night with Ella, complete with her wading in the fountain at the end of the evening.

THURSDAY—Our firm wanted to promote a better work/life balance since we all worked a lot of hours during busy season, so during the summer months, we had Fridays off. While Ella and I had discussed biking to the beach for her birthday, she received a bit of a late invite to the river from some old college friends and asked if I minded changing plans. I said, "Nope! You're the birthday girl!"

The river was not a new vacation spot for me, but this would be my first time going with a different group of people. All the others going on the trip were from Ella's college. As she and I pulled up to a house to carpool out to Laughlin, the first guy I saw caught my eye. He had a perfect smile, was grinning from ear to ear, and I immediately thought, *He is beautiful.* It was only a thought as I wasn't about to put moves on any of Ella's friends. But this guy was cute and had eyes that were bright blue, making it virtually impossible to look away.

I stepped outside of the vehicle to say hi and introduce myself.

"Hi. I'm Jude," he said with a grin.

"Nice to meet you! I've only heard great things!" I said, "I'm Heidi."

We piled into the Suburban for our four-hour drive: it was Ella, Jude, another tall guy, me, and a couple that were connected at the hip. We arrived in Laughlin late that night and went straight to bed.

FRIDAY—The next morning, we set out for Lake Mohave. It's the same lake I had been going to for the last few years. The routine was pretty similar: load up the boat with waters, ice, and beer; arrive at the launch point; and try to be some of the first ones on the water to wakeboard on the smooth, glass-like surface before the lake got busy.

After some wakeboarding, they steered the boat toward Gasoline Alley where there were cliffs for jumping. It must be a popular spot because this is where I had been with my college friends many times before. They pulled the boat into the cove, turned off the motor, and we coasted. With my life vest already on, I grabbed a beer to take with me and jumped in the water.

Three of us made our way up to the top where there were some solid jumping points. In my haste I forgot my flip-flops for the climb. The little rocks pressing into the bottoms of my feet on my way to the top were piercing, so I moved quickly. Jude, surprised at my bravery, egged me on, saying, "No way you're going to jump off the top!"

Who was this guy? Clearly, he didn't know me at all. I replied, "Of course I am! Not like I haven't done it before!" I got to my spot, shotgunned my beer, and jumped thirty feet into the water below. Jude and the other guy followed shortly after.

After a day on the lake and some flirting (which came from Jude's end more than mine), we all headed back to the hotel. The boys were going to the casino to gamble before we would meet back up and head to dinner. The three of us girls stayed in the room to take showers and get ready. The other two were in the bathroom curling their hair, and I was sitting on the edge of the bed putting my sandals on. Jude ran back in the room to grab something, but before heading back out the door, he stopped and kissed me on the forehead.

Surprised, the only thing that came to my mind and out of my mouth was, "That's it?"

Jude then responded to my question with a real kiss. On the lips.

Well. *That* was unexpected.

About an hour later, we met up with the boys to head to Chili's for dinner. The restaurant was running their "2 for $20" deal where you could order an appetizer and two meals for $20. The two lovebirds who were inseparable coupled up for the promotion, then the tall cutie and Ella were the second pair. Jude looked across the table at me and asked, "You wanna be my date?"

"Of course!" I said, sealing the deal with a smile.

Jude followed up by asking, "So, since we're a couple can I start calling you babe?"

"No."

This was my involuntary response. After hearing Chloe and her couch-surfer boyfriend use it day in and day out, it burned my ears.

"Okay, then is it all right if I call you boo?" he asked.

I laughed and nodded, saying yes in response.

And it stuck.

SATURDAY—We had another early morning on the lake and that evening went to the bowling alley. Afterward, we walked to the top of Laughlin where we had a view overlooking the river and could see the city lights. We broke into couples as we scaled up the large hill, and I chatted with Jude.

"So," I asked him, "what's your one wish?"

He answered immediately: "To make a difference in someone's life."

His quick answer gave me chills. *That was my wish*, I thought.

He explained, "I've always wanted to be a fireman. In that profession, you typically encounter people on the worst day of their life. I want to be the person to help make a difference on someone's worst day and turn it around for the better."

His response was well-thought-out and meaningful. *I also wanted to make a difference in someone's life!* I thought. Yet I still felt as though I was in the trenches of discovering what that was exactly. Back then, I had hoped it would be through the book I dreamed of writing someday or maybe by teaching yoga.

"Interesting," I replied. "That's my same wish."

Throughout the weekend, we were all on the same group text. I only had Ella's number, so I was able to figure out who was who by what was said. Since my number was the only new number for Jude, he started to text me on the side almost immediately. We also had a moment at Loser's Lounge when Jude came over to me on the dance floor, threw up his arms, and shook his hips inviting my attention. It was a carefree and fun weekend, but I didn't want to read anything into this still fledgling relationship with Jude since I had clearly misjudged similar situations in the past.

Ella and I returned to Newport after the weekend at the river, and I was headed home from a client that Monday when my phone rang. I looked down and saw it was Jude calling. Confused, since it seemed as though most people who tried to get ahold of me simply sent a text, I thought something may be urgent, so I picked up.

"Hello?"

"Hey! Heidi? It's Jude!"

"Hi . . ." I responded. *Maybe I forgot something?* I thought. *Or something was wrong.*

"How was your day?" he asked.

Was he really calling me to ask me about my day?

We talked the rest of my hour-long drive home. The next day, Jude called me at the same time once again. On this call, he asked if I wanted to go to an Angels baseball game with him on Thursday, just two days later. Surprised at his request, I told him that I needed to check my calendar and get back to him.

When I arrived home, Ella was sitting on the couch, eating dinner and watching a show. When a commercial came on, I asked about her day, then told her how Jude called me on Monday to say hi.

"Oh yeah, he's been talking to me, too," she responded as she intently fast-forwarded through the commercials.

I was trying to feel it out to ask for her permission to go to the Angels game with him. Then, I went for it.

"Jude called me again today. He invited me to go to an Angels game. Is it okay if I go?"

She turned to me with a surprised look on her face. "Of course it is! You're so sweet to ask me."

I sent him a text: *I'm free Thursday to go to the game!*

Cool! I'm excited! He responded.

I wondered if this would be considered our first date. As the thought ran through my head, he followed up his text with another: *My best friend and brother-in-law will also be there.*

Okay, cool! I responded.

And my mom, his next text said.

Okay :), I replied.

Then I received another text.

And my grandma.

When I arrived at the stadium, I stepped out of my car in my white Converse shoes and put my Angels hat on. I grabbed my purse, closed the car door, and listened for the beep when I clicked the automatic lock button. I thought to myself, *Well, here goes nothing.*

At the game I met a lot of key people in Jude's life. In addition to the four people he told me would be there, one of his aunts was working at the stadium as an usher, so I met her, too. I later learned how he thought he might as well toss me into the deep end with the people in his life to see if I would sink or swim.

The next day, I woke up to a text from Jude that read, *Good Morning, Beautiful.* This continued every morning for the next week. When I asked him how long he was going to keep this up, he replied, *Forever!* <3

Next Jude invited me down to Newport Beach where his parents were staying for a few nights. We walked to the pier and enjoyed milkshakes. He was still living at home and working part time while volunteering as a reserve fireman and applying to departments to be a paid firefighter.

The next weekend was also spent together; we went shopping at some outlet stores and grabbed dinner. It felt a little weird. We were doing things that couples do, something I hadn't done in what felt like forever. Here I was with an amazing guy, and it was all surprisingly easy. There was no chase and there was never a question of "Is he into me?" Here he was, wanting to spend all his free time with me, and we were rearranging our schedules to be together.

We made plans to go to San Diego for a weekend and stay with one of his aunts who lived in Point Loma. I already heard endless stories about how much fun his family had there together over the years.

About halfway through our drive down, as we neared Oceanside, I thought of Zach. I heard he had relocated to the San Diego area. As I gazed out the window and looked out across the Pacific Ocean while we headed south on the I-5 freeway, I hesitantly brought up the topic of exes to Jude for the first time.

I told him about my first love and how he lived in San Diego with his wife and child. It felt unusual to tell the story out loud because I hadn't spoken of it to anyone since it happened. Everyone in my life had known who Zach was, and it didn't warrant any further explanation. Yet I felt I should be up front with Jude about the one person I ever had profound feelings for in my life, and I also felt a bit on edge that I would run into him at some point, being that we now both lived in Southern California.

After my short recap of the story escaped my mouth, Jude reciprocated with the fact that his ex-girlfriend *also* lived in San Diego.

"Oh!" I said.

He told me about how this girl broke his heart years ago and that his most recent girlfriend wasn't very independent. "You're very different from her. It was crazy how that first river trip, you were in a Suburban with four people you had never met, yet you were the one driving the conversation," he said.

Feeling embarrassed, I said, "Sorry, maybe I was too much too quick."

"No," he assured me. "By the end of that four-hour drive, it was as though you were everyone's new best friend. I like that about you. I like how you're teaching Children's Church, training for a marathon, and that you're a big sister. You're motivated and doing what you can to make the world a better place."

Blushing, I responded, "Thanks. I'm definitely far from perfect."

"Well, to me, you are," he countered.

As Long as You Love Me

Six weeks later, we were officially dating. We met Ella, Chloe, and her couch-surfer boyfriend at Sharkeez for drinks that day. Chloe was skeptical about Jude and us being official, so she started quizzing him about me. I felt a little bad for Jude being put on the spot with Chloe's questions.

"What's her favorite color?" she asked.

"Yellow," he responded confidently.

"What's Heidi's dream?"

"To write a book."

She continued to drill him about me, but to my surprise, he got the big and little ones correct without hesitation and no second-guesses needed. When Chloe gave up, I think even she was shocked. He was paying attention to the details when it came to my likes, dislikes, and dreams.

The following weekend, I was Jude's date to his best friend's wedding. The duo had been friends since they were in diapers. While on the dance floor, the bride came over and gave me a big hug. I thanked her for allowing me to be Jude's plus one on such short notice.

"Of course! Jude told me, 'This one is different,' so I said bring her!"

"Oh?!" I replied with a smile. "Is that so . . .?"

Heading in the Right Direction

That Thanksgiving, my dad told me his business was doing well and he could use some help in the office. He anticipated me working for him a couple hours a week in addition to my accounting job. After hearing the update on his company, it didn't take even five minutes for a thought to enter my mind: *I can quit my job, go to Bikram Yoga Teacher Training, teach yoga, and work for my dad.*

Bikram Yoga Teacher Training was put on during the spring and fall each year. The spring session felt too soon, since it was only five months away and I would have to come up with thousands of dollars to pay for my certification and stay, so it felt more attainable to attend in the fall. This would give me time to tie up loose ends at work, take my vacations, figure out my living situation, and then peace out on accounting.

As soon as I plotted my exit plan, I let my yoga studio owners know my timeline and started doing work trade at two local studios. Work trade allowed me to help out at the front desk and clean the studio in exchange for free yoga classes.

I tried to take class that summer as often as I could to be ready for double days, little sleep, and delving into the dialogue at training. One evening, after taking class and showering at the studio, I talked with my instructor, who was behind the front desk, and thanked him for class. We started chatting, and the discussion turned into me telling him I would be attending teacher training in less than two months. From that moment, our conversation felt like it lit on fire.

"Oh really?! Congratulations, that's great!" He told me how he *also* left his corporate career to become a teacher and never regretted it. "You're going to be thrilled with your career change and absolutely love it," he assured me.

Any teacher I spoke with about training had a twinkle in their eye. I knew it was something special and the opportunity of a lifetime. So many students had to put their lives on hold for nine weeks, paid a good chunk of money, figured out living situations, and would even leave their children and spouses at home to become certified to teach Bikram yoga.

He ended our conversation with this: "If you ever need anything or help with the dialogue just let me know. Soon enough, you'll be one of us."

One of them? I thought. *How can he be so certain? Would I be able to teach a class as well as they all did?*

The teachers I interacted with all seemed to have their lives figured out and had achieved a sense of inner peace, as you would expect a yoga teacher to have. Although it felt out of reach for me, I decided I would put my best foot forward.

That summer was the most-talked-about trip to the river, complete with a keg on the dock and yoga in the kitchen. After that was our week-long beach camping trip in Mexico, where we would camp in tents for a week without a shower. We played games or laid out on the sand all day, chose to start each day with a shot at 11:07 a.m. (no matter how we felt that morning), and every evening, we would walk to the opposite side of the peninsula and watch the sunset over the ocean. It felt like paradise with a group of twenty of our friends. The biggest decision we had to make each day was what swimsuit to wear.

Jude started his first fire job working weekends, while I worked my 9 to 5 job during the week. With our opposite schedules and miles between us, he would often come to Newport during the weeknights to spend time with me. It was all coming together: dating Jude, a plan to finally quit my job, and attending training to be a yoga teacher! First, I would have a fun-filled weekend with the Tinky Winkies, fly back to SoCal for my last few days of work, enjoy my quitting party, then head to training in LA. Everything felt perfect.

Except that's not exactly how it went.

Part 4

Nothing can steal happiness, peace, away from you:
if anyone does make you angry, you are the loser;
if someone can allow you to lose peace, you are the loser.

—Bikram Choudhury

13

Caterpillar

I was feeling on top of the world heading to see the Tinky Winkies for the long weekend. We had plans to go wine tasting, attend nice dinners, and lounge by the water. Just being together was limitless fun and nonstop catching up and reminiscing, but after my arrival and some reconnecting, the conversations unexpectedly started to sting.

Ever since we were kids, Erika has been sarcastic, a great storyteller, and can take control of the room in the best way. But that weekend, it felt as if I was the butt of her jokes. *Was it just me, or would she interject negative comments after anything I said?*

A day or so into what was supposed to be our special weekend, my verdict did not change. I felt uneasy. My trips back home had become more scarce, and she saw me for only a handful of days each year. I wasn't sure what had shifted between us since I was a bridesmaid in her wedding just two summers before. She was my longest—and one of my closest—friends.

Our second day into our trip, as we all sat around chatting, it felt like she was hurling verbal darts at me as if I was the obvious target. I stepped out onto the balcony with a view of the water and sat down to take in the freshness of the summer air. I gazed at the boats speeding by, and the sun made the crystal-clear lake shimmer. It was stunning here and the best time of year to visit. It seemed as though everyone else at the lake was enjoying their holiday weekend. *Don't let it get to you*, I assured myself.

Our last night together, after arriving home from a picturesque dinner, we played a silly game, where she made the hypothetical comment, "Well, I would never want to be married to Heidi."

All right, I thought. *I'm not imagining this. She said it loud and clear.* I couldn't think of another person in my life saying something this hurtful, whether it was for a playful game or not.

I headed to the kitchen to start cleaning up and to avoid any more insults thrown my way. I retaliated: "Well, I wouldn't want to be *your* husband because all you do is complain about your life."

The room was silent, and within a few minutes we all went to bed.

The next morning, we packed up to leave and head our separate ways. I was giving all the girls hugs goodbye when Erika retreated to the other side of her car, got in with a wave, and left.

Why didn't I just stand up for myself from the beginning?

I was mad at myself for handling the situation poorly. I ran the weekend through my mind over and over on the car ride to Seattle before I would fly back to California the following morning. Something about *me* bothered Erika. She didn't like me suggesting we go on a hike. She didn't like the places I recommended for dinner. She didn't like the color of a bridesmaid dress that I said I envisioned having for *my* future wedding. *What was different now between us and why?*

Upon returning home, I was devastated how this "perfect weekend" I envisioned ended up. I also couldn't shake all the terrible feelings I felt about myself. I talked to Ella about what had happened and the words that were said. I wanted someone else's opinion. *Was I truly a terrible friend and no one had the guts to tell me?* Ella and I had lived together for three years now, so if anyone would know how I am day in and day out, it would be her.

After I word vomited to Ella about the events and comments from the weekend and showed her additional text messages, I felt sick. *What if I* am *awful?* I previously prided myself in being a good friend, but maybe I am that dense and haven't a clue.

When Ella finally looked up at me after reading what I showed her, she said, "None of what she said describes the Heidi I know at all. Honestly. I think she's holding on to something from the past."

I breathed a sigh of relief. It felt like everyone else at that moment in my life was illuminating positivity and cheering me on for the big changes I was about to make. I knew I shouldn't dwell on this one opinion, no matter how heavily it weighed on my heart and how important and intertwined she had always been in my life.

People advise you that your childhood or high school friends are likely not your forever friends. Up until this moment, I frequently gloated that I had defied the odds and continued to prove the statement false. But as life goes on, it is inevitable that you cannot stay in touch with every friend you have ever made. It's natural for friendships to evolve. Sometimes there's an obvious reason for changes in the relationship, but sometimes it isn't as apparent as you would hope it to be.

Oftentimes, there is a season or a specific reason that friends we encounter are a part of our life. While I had heard this and knew it could apply to my life at some point, I never thought *this* friendship would change. Couldn't I choose a different one from whom to grow apart? Maybe I had painted the memories of an exquisite relationship better in my mind than what was now my reality. Maybe I missed the imperfections and chose to hold onto the shining moments. Maybe I forgot the dark times and remembered only the bright ones. I somehow must have missed the whole picture.

So here it was, when I thought everything would be perfect: I was supposed to finish the summer on a high note. But that wasn't how it went. My heart was crushed and it made the events that followed bittersweet, but I moved forward. I had held my breath waiting for everything in my life to fall perfectly in its place, but I've learned that sometimes we hold out for those moments, and they might never arrive.

The End

Quitting my job was hands down one of the *best* days of my life to date. I completed my exit interview with our sweet Human Resources gal, turned in my laptop, and left the office with a huge smile on my face. As I hurried to the elevator, the joy circulating through my body was undeniable. I wanted to avoid any final forced conversation with anyone at the firm since I was now unemployed and wanted to dodge a potentially awkward interaction.

This accounting job helped me pay off school, my car, my bills for me to live in Newport Beach, and it paid for my yoga training. I seniored my public company audit that year and was ready to close the chapter of me working in the corporate world after four years at my firm. From this moment on, my firm could not legally reach out to me for anything further. There would no longer be emails on Friday evenings asking for something first thing in the morning. No more auditing checklists, no more pressure to pass the CPA exam, and no more staying up to date on accounting standards.

I was *free*.

That evening, my friends and newly ex-coworkers went out to celebrate my last day of work. Then, on Sunday, I loaded up my car and headed to LA, where I would be for the next nine weeks of yoga training.

The Yoga Education

That first week was a challenge mentally. We had two yoga classes every day of the week, with just one on Saturday mornings and no class on Sundays. I was pushing my body to the limit, going to posture clinics, listening to lectures from Bikram, and squeezing in memorizing dialogue with any free time that was left over.

Each trainee was assigned a group number. These same numbers would determine which line you were on in the massive ballroom where we practiced yoga. We would rotate from the very front, where we had full visibility of ourselves in the mirror, to the back, where we would have no visibility to assist with balance or alignment. Our yoga room had rows of colorful mats on the floor and an intense, overwhelming heat that seemed hotter than ever before.

During my first week, with us all being new to the process and each other, a guy and a girl hopped into class at the very last minute and squeezed in next to me on both sides. Their mats were less than two inches from mine, both to my left and to my right. Irritated, I focused on my practice and tried to stagger with them as best as I could during the postures.

When we were more than halfway through class on the floor in *poorna salabhasana*, both of them were inadvertently holding me up as we tried to contain our laughter. Being so close to one another, I did my best to avoid extending my fingers into their eyes or armpits. It was virtually impossible to abstain from dripping sweat on each other. After class, and throughout the rest of training, the three of us became friends, and I learned the guy was from Chile and the girl was from New York.

This yoga, through the sweat and tears, connected us all, no matter what language we spoke, what life we previously lived, or what continent we were from. We were all there for the same reason: to learn how to teach a class that changed our lives for the better. It was astonishing being in a room with like-minded, motivated teachers from all over the world who were also ready to put their lives on hold for the experience.

For me, Bikram yoga provides a workout unlike any I had ever tried. The practice is designed to assist in deepening the mind-body connection, and it helped me develop the necessary tools to deal with anxiety, whether through breathing cues practiced or the self-love I developed. In life, we can put ourselves on autopilot and be completely unaware and oblivious to our surroundings, but I've learned in yoga to exhale the desire to control and inhale what is there waiting for me when I am open to the possibilities.

While at training in Los Angeles, Jude was sent on a fire strike team for work and then forced to work multiple days thereafter.

We knew we would likely have to go quite a while without seeing each other. After a few weeks into my training, he was finally on one of his first breaks home. He came straight to LA to see me after we spent more than fifty days apart. It felt so special to have him there, supporting my dreams.

Once he arrived, he agreed to take class with me since guests were allowed to drop in with the trainees. He had to practice in the back of the large ballroom with other teachers and staff, while I was on my designated line. The timing of his arrival at my training was a day or two after the room reached such a high heat, the fire sprinklers had burst during class. Days subsequent to the deluge, the room did not reach its normal heated level. So while the room was a bit cooler than normal, Jude's teacher was a former Olympian, so I thought he might still be impressed with the class.

"What did you think of it?" I asked him in the lobby afterward.

"It wasn't that hard nor very hot," he responded.

"Well, yeah, that was by far the coolest class so far!" I exclaimed. Of course he would luck out after the heat broke for the weekend.

It was so nice to have him there with me. He met my roommate and the close friends I had made. He saw what my life looked like staying in that hotel for nine weeks. He saw it all firsthand, and most importantly, he was *proud* of me.

We soon said our goodbyes with a kiss and a prolonged hug. I would see him again in another week or so, and I knew this remaining time apart would be worth it.

Previous to attending training, yoga had helped me to lose weight, reduce stress, and have better control of my emotions. It also gave me the conviction that there was *no* obstacle in yoga or life that was too big to overcome.

This aligned with why I wanted to become a yoga teacher: I wanted to help others overcome whatever obstacles they had created in their own minds or to regain the confidence they may have previously lost and choose to believe in themselves. I wanted to be alongside them through their journey to cheer them on. My process of defying the odds and ignoring my self-limiting beliefs reached a whole new level the day Bikram put me on the spot in class.

The Moment

About halfway through training, it was my group's turn to be in the third row. We had class that morning, and I arrived a bit later than usual to the 5 p.m. class. I placed my mat down in the only open area on my assigned line, eerily close to the stage, which I normally avoided like the plague. The closer to the stage you were, the more likely you would be in Bikram's line of sight. He would often give students direct instructions, putting them on the spot, and his class could sometimes go as long as two-and-a-half hours instead of the normal ninety minutes.

Anytime we walked in the room, we knew he was teaching if his leopard towel was draped over the chair. That evening it was.

He began class as he always did with his dialogue: "Bend your body right and left and right and left and right and left!" paired with whatever was on his mind that day. Toward the middle of class, we were standing in separate leg stretching pose. In this posture, you take a four-foot lateral step, extend your arms out to both sides, bend your body forward at the lower spine, then grab your heels and touch your forehead to the floor. For the last few years practicing this posture, I told myself there was no way I would ever get my forehead to touch the floor.

At my home studio, a lot of the shorter ladies in class would get into the posture with ease. I confirmed in my mind that I was tall, would never be that flexible, and "touching your forehead to the floor" was more a figure of speech than an actuality for me.

Once his instructions began, I attempted to the best of my ability, as I always did, to lengthen my spine and get my forehead to the floor.

"Miss Yellow. Miss Yellow!"

Bikram was trying to get someone's attention.

I realized I was wearing yellow, and that someone was *me*.

Startled, I stood up, and my eyes met his. From the stage he started to give the instructions again. It was exactly what the posture had always been. Take a four-foot step, go down from the lower spine, grab your heels from the outside (five fingers together!), lengthen your spine, and touch your forehead to the floor. Once there was a lull in his instructions, other students started to get into the posture and he replied, "No, no. Just Miss Yellow."

I paused, then took a deep breath and got into the posture like he said, as I had always tried before, and as I had always known it to be.

"Widen your feet. More. More. More." He continued, "Nice tight grip, now pull your heels as hard as possible. Chin up, head up, roll forward like a wheel. Touch your forehead to the floor. Your forehead should touch the floor. Roll forward like a wheel. Roll forward!"

I tried my best as everyone watched me attempt a posture I had never successfully achieved. In the middle of his directions, he made the comment: "If you're going to be a teacher, you need to touch your forehead to the floor!"

No way, I thought. *He's not going to stop. I have to give up because I'm not even close. What should I do? This is so embarrassing.*

With all the yogis' eyes on me, I did the best I could for what felt like forever but was likely less than three minutes of hearing his words and him calling me "Miss Yellow." I gripped my heels, shifted my weight to my toes, lengthened my spine, and then, I touched my forehead to the floor for the very first time in my life. I was in utter shock. Everybody started cheering, so I stood up straight. Bikram was clapping! He gave me a smirk and casually went on to teach the next posture.

I was floored. I just made what had been previously impossible, possible.

This was my breakthrough. It wasn't just successfully completing the posture, but it was what I needed: knowing that there was nothing unattainable as long as I worked hard and believed in myself. Bikram picked me out of the 314 trainees in the hot room that day and gave me exactly what I needed. He saw my potential.

The hope this training instills in the trainees and the fulfillment it brought specifically to me was undeniable. We completed ninety-nine classes that ranged anywhere from 1.5 to 2.5 hours in length. If you do the math, every yogi would have spent a minimum of approximately 150 hours in the hot room in those short nine weeks. Everything from the practice—the man, the people, the staff, the repetitiveness, the immersion, the breakthroughs, the enlightenment, the smells, the lack of sleep, your changing body, and your new home—plays a part in your willingness to trust the process and see what is on the other side of letting go.

The Man

Bikram was the first to implement hot classes in the United States. He crafted the sequence of twenty-six postures and two breathing exercises, and he also encouraged studios to keep their yoga room heated to 105 degrees with 40 percent humidity.

Bikram yoga earned its once stellar reputation for bringing improved health and hope to Los Angeles. Unfortunately, the story took a sad turn as this man also abused his power and people in the process. He brought such an amazing, restorative, and healing practice, yet he self-sabotaged his own empire.

Toward the end of training, I stepped onto the elevator and found myself sharing the space with Bikram and six other people. He was dressed up all in white.

"Wow, Bikram!" I exclaimed. "You're looking fresh!"

He smirked, furrowed his brow, and replied to my compliment with, "Fresh? What is fresh? I look *fresh*?"

While it is a figure of speech, it is obvious this man, who is flawed and well misunderstood, is also finding his place in this world.

It was an interesting time for me to attend training before his empire went downhill, but I am utterly grateful it went exactly that way. Even so, this yoga brought so much light to my life, peace to my heart, and genuine friendships for my soul.

The Beginning

After an effortless transition home after yoga training, I had so much to look forward to and it all happened refreshingly without stress. During my training, a friend of Ella's agreed to rent my room for a short three months while I was living in Los Angeles, which pushed into the holidays. It was another telling reminder that when something is meant to happen, everything will fall into place.

Soon, I moved back into my apartment, was teaching yoga, and working for my dad, meaning I could wear yoga pants to both jobs and no makeup. I was settling into my new role that Thanksgiving. It was crazy how, the previous year, I had decided on Thanksgiving Day to quit my job, go to training, and work for my dad. And here I was, a year later, with it all happening and feeling even better than how I imagined it would.

A lot of my close friends realized how normal I still was even after attending yoga training. I learned that some of them were nervous I would return home spiritually connected to the earth or choose to stop shaving my armpits.

Needless to say, neither of those assumptions came to fruition.

At training, I lost weight and was the fittest I had been since double practice days for volleyball at college. Not only was there a noticeable difference on the outside, but, on the inside, I was shifting toward the inner peace I desperately needed. Here I was, a caterpillar happily moving along in life, yet I could feel in my mind, body, and soul that something was changing within me. Although I felt the most content I had ever been, we all well know, a caterpillar goes through messy developmental stages before its huge transformation into a butterfly.

14

Falling Out

The girls were all dressed in sequins and the boys in button-ups and dress pants, ringing in the new year. The house was decorated with glittering décor and a shimmering disco ball. It was special to have all of Jude's and my friends at the same party, counting down until midnight with our champagne flutes in hand. We were celebrating the year coming to a close. It was the year I made the biggest leap of faith and never looked back. Everything felt like it was in the right place, and, most importantly, I felt like *I* was in the right place.

The new year brought on teaching nine classes a week and getting well acquainted with my dad's company. I was busy, still putting in a lot of hours, but they weren't as stressful as they had been before. I felt lighter and happier and had much more yoga in my life. But that also meant I was continuing to work hard not only at my new jobs but also on myself.

In Bikram yoga, we use the term "falling out" to describe when you start to lose your balance, your grip, and accidentally come out of a posture earlier than desired or anticipated. You may lose focus in the mirror, your muscles can start to shake, or maybe you're kicking, stretching, or bending too hard and too far. You need to come back to your concentration, meditation, stillness, alignment, and breath to regain your composure before starting again.

Falling out, however, is how you test your limits. If you were to practice yoga a few days a week for the rest of your life and never fall out of a posture, you're likely doing it wrong. When you kick too high or push yourself so far that you lose your grip in class (or in *life*), you can feel disappointed. However, falling out, and essentially falling down, is part of the process. If you don't push yourself, you will never know your potential. Sometimes, falling short or even failing is what makes us stand back up stronger than before.

Jude and I got in a rhythm of coordinating our schedules as best we could, but there started to be some friction. There were times he voiced how he would rather be home an extra night to hit the gym in the morning before coming to see me. Or he would choose to play softball with his friends during that one small sliver of time we could see each other during the week. It started to feel like I was taking a back seat, and it was occurring more frequently than before.

That March, Jude and I were invited to a wedding by a couple we met through his friends. I knew a total of eight people at the event.

After the ceremony was over and the reception began, I asked Jude to join me on the dance floor. He denied my request, which was disappointing.

How had he been so much fun and danced with me the weekend we met at the river but not now?

I knew it was somewhere inside of him, yet he seemed resistant and put in little effort to make me feel important that night. So I found one of the only couples I knew and hung out with them on the dance floor.

After working up a sweat from all the dancing, I went to find Jude, who was hanging out and casually laughing with the guys, oblivious to what I was up to. He knows I can hold my own, but after over an hour apart from your date, it would have been nice for him to check on me instead of assuming I was fine.

Annoyed, I pulled him aside and said, "Hey, I'm not usually needy or anything, but I've been on the dance floor without you while you've been content hanging with your friends."

"Why are you mad that I'm hanging out with my friends?" he snapped back.

We started to argue when I questioned how he was treating me. Being at a wedding quickly turned to the topic of marriage. He got irritated at the mention of it and said, "I'm not even sure it's you."

Stunned, I left the party with one of the other girls soon after he made the comment and sobbed in her truck as she tried to console me. I also contemplated having a friend come pick me up from the event, even though we had plans to stay that night. It was the girl who convinced me to stay when I was certain I wanted to leave.

Jude had led me to believe that "this one is different." After just months of dating, I had been invited to Cancun with his family for their annual trip. That's when he mentioned that I was the "exception," meaning their family didn't typically allow for just any boyfriend or girlfriend to join a family vacation. From the get-go, he let me know I was the type of girl he wanted to marry. But it felt as though the narrative changed, and here I was, completely caught off-guard.

Jude waited until the afternoon of the next day to address our discussion the night before. He said he was sorry if he hurt my feelings and reassured me that he never intended to make me feel unimportant. He confirmed that he loved me; this was just our first big fight. Even after hearing his comforting words, it did not mean things were fine for me.

Am I wasting my time? What changed from when he met me until now?

We were a year and a half into our relationship, lived over an hour apart, and I had rearranged my life to be with him. I understand if someone isn't ready for marriage, but what I didn't understand was being with someone if they didn't want to marry them.

Was this all for nothing?

Everything had been lining up in my life, but this was a blow to my reality.

Back in Newport, I still had my social circle and was eager to get my mind off the situation. I went out with my friends, put on a smile, and acted unfazed. I knew that I could break up with Jude and go back to this life, but I also knew he was too great of a guy to let go of that easily. It pierced my heart to picture us being over and him dating someone else. I wanted to be with Jude, but I also didn't know how long I wanted to wait for him to figure out that he wanted to be with me too.

On a day when I felt at my lowest, I found my way into a yoga class. One of my fellow teachers chatted between the first and second set of camel pose while we were lying down in *savasana.* Camel pose is one of the deepest backward bends in the Bikram sequence and is also known to open up the front of your body, including your heart. I could feel mine racing as she said, "Obstacles are often put in our life for a reason: to see how much fight we have within us or to discover how much something truly means to us . . ."

It was the reminder I needed. My eyes welled up with tears, not knowing how long I would need to surmount the huge hurdle in front of me.

While I knew Jude and my timelines were slightly off, him a bit younger and me contemplating marriage sooner than he was, I also knew there was so much beauty in the chance that this relationship could be forever, and it was worth the effort to find out. If everything came to me easily, I wouldn't appreciate it as much as I should. If I chose to fight through resistance or struggles, it's an indicator that whatever it is would be something worth fighting for. I've learned that often there will be barriers that block the end goal or a magnificent view.

My friends told me to break up with Jude. Not because they didn't like him but because they loved me and wanted me to be happy. It irritated me that he wasn't sure about me. Like taking a cold shower or getting into bed with the sheets untucked. It made my skin crawl. Months had gone by since he made the comment, and I didn't know how many more months I would wait.

I attempted to keep myself busy and my mind off my timeline with Jude. I said yes to hanging out with friends every opportunity I got. I jam-packed fun into my life between concerts, river trips, participating in a thirty-day yoga challenge, completing my second marathon, spending more time with my little sister, and attending bachelorette parties and weddings. Yet the bittersweet feeling remained since things felt on the rocks with Jude.

Well, love wasn't working out for me, but it was for Lucas. A few months prior, I received an invitation to his wedding. He and I hadn't been as close as we were when we were younger, especially now that we both had significant others. I was thrilled for him: he and his fiancé planned to have a low-key celebration, and once he told me the date, I immediately looked at last-minute flights, which were expensive.

My dad was displeased when I approached him to request the time off, just weeks after I started working for him. The wedding would be during one of our busiest and most profitable times of the year.

It tugged on my heart.

Reluctantly, I let Lucas know I couldn't make it on such short notice at such a busy time. My decline to his wedding invitation didn't feel like me. I wanted to be there to support him just like he had always done for me. I was bummed to miss out on his big day.

Luckily, he and his wife road-tripped down to California for their honeymoon, so I took them out to sushi to celebrate their big step in life! I thought they made a great match. She was younger than him but mature for her age. She was more calm and easygoing than other girls he dated, and I thought they complemented each other well. Lucas deserved someone amazing, and I was so happy he found her.

The Bottom Line

At the end of the year, I was getting receipts and paperwork together for taxes. I completed my first full year teaching yoga and working for my dad after leaving my well-paying job. And when I compared my income levels with my bottom line, my eyes got huge: I made thousands of dollars less than the previous year, but my income came out even.

How did I maintain this Newport life and still afford everything?!

My taxable income was lower, my rent was less after moving into a cheaper condo, and a lot of my free time was spent teaching or taking yoga class instead of going out with friends. It reinforced the fact that money would not equate to a happy life if my heart isn't in it. And no amount of money is worth forfeiting how you feel inside.

A few weeks later, I had a final call with one of the Big Brothers Big Sisters representatives to answer some follow-up questions and essentially close out my file. Erika and I were matched when she was fourteen years old; the program technically lasted until she completed high school or turned eighteen, and we had hit the end of that time. But even after she graduated, we could still meet up and stay connected.

The rep asked what I liked most about being a big sister, if I would recommend the agency to others, or if I had any additional feedback for her.

My little sister and I got along straight away and had inside jokes after our first time hanging out. We consistently met up one to two times a month and had fun going to the movies, ice skating, having beach days or sleepovers. The woman on the phone and I chatted for a bit, and she closed by telling me, "Well, Erika loved having you as a big sister."

"Oh! Great!" I said.

"I had this same call with her. She made it sound like you two still plan to hang out."

"Yes, we have some hangouts on the calendar." I said.

The reality of it was, my Little felt like family to me, so I planned to continue spending time with her.

"That's great," she responded. "I asked her what she liked about having you as a big sister. She said she had a lot of fun with you, that you were gracious with your time, and that you gave really great advice."

"Oh really?" I asked, a bit surprised.

"Yes, she said that when you first met her when she was a freshman, you told her to not pay attention to or worry about boys. She said you also told her they will likely be a waste of time so to stick to her girlfriends. She said that's exactly what she did."

The woman's words made me smile. I felt so proud of my little sister. I had a great high school experience with my girlfriends and didn't need a guy to fill my time back then. Now here I was, at a point in my life when I was looking for my forever person and still didn't want to be wasting my time.

Part 5

There's so much magic in each and every day,
and it's all how we choose to see it.

—Unknown

15

#BALLERSTATUSCELEBRATIONS

Ella's birthday was at the tail end of summer and became the annual excuse for the girls to get together and drink champagne. Even though Chloe had moved back to Northern California, it felt like she still lived down south because she was always in attendance at the big events. Things were rocky with the couch-surfer guy, but she was down for the rendezvous with the girls. She needed us. And I obviously needed her.

We kicked off the fun-filled weekend with a wine bar, then some sushi, and dancing the following evening with the whole crew. It felt just like old times with the couch surfer and Chloe sitting rather close, and our old guy roommates were also there. We were back together just like we had been in that big house as a little family.

After arriving home from our evening, Ella discovered she had misplaced her phone. We logged into "Find My iPhone" on her laptop, only to discover it was on the 55 South Freeway, heading back into Newport Beach, still in the taxicab. Four of us jumped in the car, chased down the taxi, and retrieved her phone in dramatic fashion. That same weekend, we even surprised Ella with a Taylor Swift "1989" concert ticket, making the weekend absolutely epic. Everything was grand aside from my love life.

I started to hit my limit with Jude. It felt as though he took for granted what we had, and I wanted him to experience life without me again. That, I told myself, would be a telling sign if we were meant to be together or not.

I asked him to meet halfway for me to give him his stuff back, but he convinced me otherwise. So I did what I did in years past: I packed my bag and headed down to San Diego. I was a professional at distracting myself when something wasn't right, and San Diego provided that magical breath of fresh air I needed.

I stayed with one of my friends from Pacific Academy, and we went out that night to the beach town where she lived to grab a drink. We started at a rooftop with an ocean view. As we moved from place to place, we could hear the echo of the waves in the background of our conversations paired with the salt on our skin. The ocean air ignited my natural curls though I had straightened my hair for the evening.

I'm not sure if it was the water nearby or the fact that we were in San Diego; whatever it was, I felt more at ease with myself than I had for a long time. I needed space to clear my mind from my disappointment with Jude.

At our first stop, a guy approached my friend, and they started talking. Shortly after, we were introduced to their pack of four boys. My friend had recently had an engagement called off after eight years of dating, so, needless to say, she was in her "yes" year . . . and flirting was something she was not choosing to shy away from.

One of the other guys took to me instantly. It felt abnormal, as I wasn't trying to entertain anything nor was looking for attention. I had the one I wanted, but I was also sitting in his waiting room for an unknown amount of time wondering if he still wanted me too.

My friend and I went to another spot, and about a half-hour later, the same four boys randomly showed up and flagged us down again. That's when we started to chat. The one guy and I got on the topic of jobs, so I told him I taught yoga and worked for my dad. He told me his dad's profession was writing books, and I agreed how amazing that was, telling him that it was one of my dreams to write one.

And that's when the topic arose.

"Wow, you really have everything going for you, don't you? How are you single?" he asked.

"Actually, I have a boyfriend." I said.

"Oh, of course you do," he responded sarcastically.

Caught off guard, I replied, "What do you mean?"

"Because it seems like all the best and prettiest girls are always taken."

I didn't know how to respond.

"Uh, I'm going to grab another drink." I finally replied, breaking the awkward silence, and made my way to the bartender.

Am I holding on to nothing? I have a track record for doing exactly that. I tend to hold on to things, especially people, when it's past time to let go. Here I was, putting my life on hold, endlessly waiting for Jude. It was as if I was on a train ride with no stops preplanned and the arrival time at the final destination was unknown. Or, even worse, we would never even *get* there. I'm just sitting here on this train, waiting in faith for it to stop at my desired location.

I saw Jude the next day. I wanted to tell him about my weekend and admit to him that I was at the end of my rope because when that guy asked for my number at the end of the night, it crossed my mind to give it to him. But Jude kept telling me to wait. Any time he knew I was contemplating breaking up, he wouldn't let it happen. I knew that the potential of what could be far outweighed the current overwhelm I felt about our disconnected timelines. The possibility of "us" being together forever felt worthwhile and more important than the hurt I felt toward him in that moment of time.

The next month, Lauren FaceTimed me to tell me she was engaged to her new boyfriend after they had been dating for six months. I was thrilled for her to find her person and honored to be asked to be her bridesmaid in the spring. Moments after feeling excitement for her, sadness quickly followed for my own situation.

Once November hit, I chose to journal sixty days of thankfulness for the holiday season to close out the year. I needed to shift my thoughts to focus on all the good in my life instead of the rockiness of my relationship with Jude. The holidays always felt like an exceptional time each year, and they could usually bring about clarity and meaning.

After returning home from a trip to Chicago to visit my sister, I spent a long weekend with Jude. We were standing in his parents' kitchen casually talking when Jude told me he planned to propose that year.

"Wait . . . *really*?!" I wasn't sure if I heard him correctly or had just wished the words in my head.

"Yup," he replied.

"But what makes you sure?" I asked.

"Well, I went and met with my old youth pastor to ask him how I should know. He told me, 'Imagine Heidi walked in the room right now, holding hands with some other guy. How would that make you feel?' I told him I would be furious. And he told me that was my answer."

I thought, *That's it? That's all it took*? But, smiling, I tried to contain my excitement and shouted, "Okay!"

Jude doesn't like to agree to things he can't commit to. Even in his daily life, his job as a fireman often made it difficult to confirm his attendance at events in case something comes up at work, making him unable to leave. When he would agree to something, there was often a disclaimer attached: "If I'm not forced to stay at work, I will be there." It was him being honest and dependable, and he didn't want me to get my hopes up, only to be let down.

Saying he was going to propose to me was no different. He told me his intention was to only get married one time in his lifetime, to one person. It's crazy to think that out of all the girls in the whole world, he chose me. He didn't give in to my sadness or tears to keep me happy or say words I wanted to hear or propose just because I wanted him to. He took his time to solidify his choice to be with me. I realized why it had never worked out with anybody else, because Jude and I were always meant to be.

The Exchange

I flew back to Lynden to be a bridesmaid in Lauren's wedding. I arrived a few days before her big day to help with last minute to-dos, then Jude flew in for the rehearsal dinner. The wedding took place in an old barn Lauren's dad helped her grandpa build before she was even born. What once housed cows was now painted white and revamped for her special event with gorgeous flowers and twinkling lights.

Once the ceremony was over, there were so many hugs from friends I hadn't seen in years. I walked over to the Tinky Winkies' moms and told them, "Jude is here! You need to meet him."

"Oh, honey, we met him already," one of the moms replied. "Everybody here has. He's practically the mayor!"

Over the years, Jude heard stories about all these people and took the initiative to go around and introduce himself. While looking for him, I ran into Lucas. He greeted me with his normal "*Heidiii*!!" and a huge hug.

"Official congrats again on being a married man!" I responded.

Lucas started talking a million miles a minute. He asked about Jude and said he wanted to meet him. He asked how California was and that he wanted to visit. He said he was stoked for Lauren and talked about the mini reunion taking place with so many old classmates in attendance.

While I was happy to see him, our interaction felt a little off. He rambled on and didn't seem his normal self or even let me squeeze in a response to any of his questions. I tried to ensure the awkwardness I felt wasn't betrayed by my facial expressions.

Just then, I felt a tug on my arm from another friend who interrupted the uncomfortable exchange.

"Aww! I met Jude! He is so great. He told me his plan to propose!" she said.

Shocked at the words that were just relayed to me, but before I could open my mouth to ask a question, I was summoned back with the wedding party, so I waved a quick goodbye to Lucas.

After the introductions were speeches, dancing, and karaoke. That's when Jude busted out his moves (which had been previously stowed away for who knows *what* reason). Later in the evening, he sang a duet with the bride's dad, whom he had just met that day. This *was* the guy I wanted to spend forever with.

Within days of being back home from our trip, Jude and I drove out to the river early to beat traffic for the holiday weekend. We swung by the store and headed over to the river house where we would wait on the dock for the other river rats to arrive.

We wore matching trucker hats to block the sun, popped open our beverages, and chatted, comfortable in the familiar surroundings and beautiful view. Returning from Lauren's wedding the week before helped to spark the conversation about what we wanted for ours. We discussed the guest list, bridesmaids, and the groomsmen: I was pinching myself we were actually having the conversation. I couldn't believe we were casually making plans for the day I had dreamed of all my life. And it all took place on the dock where Chloe and I had discussed the topic about burnt pizza, which felt so long ago.

The Question

A few weeks later, my sisters and I took a trip to Europe. We sipped champagne in France, swam in the picturesque Lake Como, saw the vast green Cliffs of Moher, and rode bikes in Amsterdam in the rain before the clouds parted and a rainbow sealed the end of our day and trip. I was no doubt living my dream life.

Upon my arrival home, Jude picked me up at LAX. I was grinning from ear to ear as we headed down to San Diego for the Fourth of July weekend.

I barely slept the entire flight home. I kept thinking that maybe he would propose at my favorite spot at Sunset Cliffs in San Diego. But I didn't want to get my hopes up, only to be let down.

When I woke up in San Diego the next morning, I felt as though hints were coming my way. His aunt insisted we go get our nails done, which she and I hadn't done before, and my friend made a comment about me retouching up my hair when it could already hold a curl, but, again, maybe I was pushing my luck.

We pulled up to Sunset Cliffs that afternoon and walked down to the edge of the large rocks where the waves were crashing. My heart was pounding. We admired the view, and each couple took their turn taking a picture with the ocean behind them.

When it was our turn, I noticed it seemed like everyone took out their phone or camera to snap a photo. I smiled next to Jude, then turned to walk away. Nothing had happened. *I knew it*! I thought. I shouldn't have gotten my hopes up.

Not a moment later, Jude was down on one knee. He looked up at me and said, "Heidi, I knew you were someone so special from the moment we met. I've enjoyed our last few years being together, and you make me the happiest guy on earth. You're my best friend, and I want to spend the rest of my life with you. Will you marry me?"

It *was* happening. And it was surreal. The pounding in my heart turned to a flutter. I felt my hands shaking out of nervousness and exhilaration. I replied, "*Yes!!*"

Everyone cheered as we kissed and hugged. I had tears in my eyes. The waiting and anticipating paid off. It was all worth it.

I would be spending forever with the person I was always meant to be with.

It Was Always You

People have often asked how I knew Jude was the one and why I held on when he wasn't sure I was his forever person. When I would think about my future with Jude, I never felt scared. I knew he would take care of me, I knew he would love me, and I knew that if we were to have a family someday, he would be all in.

It was that coupled with the three points from that sermon I heard right before I met him—spiritual unity, life-purpose compatibility, and being emotionally healthy—that confirmed it for me. I could no longer picture my life without him in it. I knew he was far too special for me to leave. Now that we were on the same page, we tied the knot.

Our wedding was held at a lovely venue near Jude's hometown. The property hosted rows of sweet orange groves as well as a hangar turned into a large livable space. After the girls enjoyed our morning mimosas paired with having our hair and makeup done, Jude and I had our first look, then we took countless pictures with the bridal party and family.

With thirty minutes to chill before we needed to line up for the ceremony, we mingled in the hangar at the venue to stay out of the heat and out of sight. The boys had tequila left over from the night before, so I asked Jude if we could take a shot and toast our wedding party. He agreed, poured the shots, rallied everyone, turned to me, and said, "Here you go, you wanted to give a toast!"

"Yes! Where's mine?" I asked.

With everyone circled around us, he handed me my shot glass, but when I opened my mouth to speak, I completely choked up. My eyes started to burn, and tears welled up, threatening to cascade down my cheeks. I physically could not get a word out. For a girl who has no trouble talking to strangers, speaking to large groups, or communicating how she feels, I was speechless.

Jude looked surprised, but he stepped in, saying, "Heidi and I just wanted to say thanks to all of you for being a part of our special day . . ."

I felt like Ariel from *The Little Mermaid.* My voice disappeared and the emotions felt overwhelming. I had planned to say, "We are so excited to celebrate our love with the people we love all together in the same place for the first time in my life. . ." But that didn't happen.

Next thing I knew, everyone chimed in at the conclusion of Jude's remarks with "Cheers!" We all clinked the colorful plastic mini glasses and drank our shots.

I panicked. If I couldn't say *that*, what about my vows?

Jude looked at me, read my mind, and reassured me, saying, "You'll be fine during the ceremony; just look at me."

When the big moment came, and I started down the aisle, I walked at a quick pace, eager to get to the front of the long stretch of grass since everyone's eyes were on me.

When I arrived at the end of the center aisle, my arm linked with my dad's, I looked up at Jude just as he told me to. I was surprised at the sight of him: he was constantly wiping away the tears that were streaming down his face. Our pastor waited a moment for Jude to pull himself together as everyone laughed. Jude was sobbing.

After I had obsessively checked the weather for two weeks before our big day, it turned out to be a high of eighty degrees with a slight breeze. What *didn't* go so well was the local AirFest happened to be that same day.

During the ceremony, our pastor paused every few minutes while the sound of airplanes drowned out his words. We both pulled ourselves together and exchanged our written vows, complete with "I do." At the reception, I had guests approach me to say "Your dress is the prettiest one I've ever seen!" or "Congrats, you and Jude make the most perfect couple," and there was also "Wow, the air show is awesome!"

In addition to the noisy airplanes that flew over us, soon a helicopter joined the ruckus and circled our venue. Jude threw his hand up and cheered while his coworkers followed suit. It was their fire crew's helicopter that had stopped by the air show, then took a special route home to fly over our event. It was undoubtedly special for Jude on top of our perfect day.

We sat down at our sweetheart table surrounded by our large wedding party: guys in navy suits, girls in champagne-colored dresses, sequin tablecloths, colorful florals, and chilled bubbles. The event was all outdoors, complete with a gorgeous sunset followed by a sky so clear you could see the stars. It was my favorite kind of night.

I got to marry my best friend, and my family and friends were there to celebrate. Guests had flown in from over twenty states, and everyone special to us was all in one place at the same time. It was something I had never experienced since moving from my hometown. We were announced as Mr. and Mrs. Fischer, made our grand entrance, and immediately dove into our first dance to "I Don't Dance" by Lee Brice. It was Jude's choice.

I wanted to pinch myself. I thought, *I am the luckiest girl in the world.*

After a handful of speeches, the dance floor was packed full of our guests overflowing onto the grass. The playlist was on point, complete with a DJ and MC who led our guests in choreographed dances.

At dusk, Jude and I were whisked off for our couples' photos in the amazing lighting that emanates at that time of day. As we took pictures in the orange groves, our photographer said, "All right, now, lean in near one another. I'll snap a few of your faces nice and close."

Jude then leaned in and kissed my forehead, just like he did the weekend we met.

Time of Our Lives

I previously had heard how hard a couple's first year of marriage can be, but for us, that wasn't the case. After our first month as husband and wife, it felt like such a privilege to live at the same place and to receive a goodbye kiss each morning, coupled with "See you tonight."

I've learned that sometimes things that are the hardest to put to words are often the most beautiful. I love Jude. We connect on a deeper level in life, and just being with him makes me feel complete. He's quick to apologize when he's wrong (which I'm still working on), and we both value communication with one another over being "right." If things feel off between us, we take the necessary steps to get them back on track. Our biggest hurdle is often the busyness of life, keeping up with social calendars of family and friends, and making time for just the two of us. I've learned that finding your "happily ever after" doesn't mean life gets easy; it just means you find the person you choose to navigate life with and commit to loving each other, no matter what comes your way.

I was checking things off my bucket list: marrying my best friend, attending a Coldplay concert, visiting Big Sur, and traveling to Europe with my husband. Jude checked off some of his goals with our trip to New York City, and he also completed his first full Ironman. We were pursuing our big dreams, both individually and as a couple, together. It felt as though I was finally whole.

16

The First Year

It's all very routine, you know. Book your flight months in advance, plan your trip, pack your bag, and check the weather for the destination spot to which you are headed. Necessities: boarding pass, ID, phone charger. Check, check, and check. *If I forget something, I can buy it, right?*

Except this time, it wasn't like that at all. This trip wasn't planned. This flight was booked hours prior to departure.

At the age of twenty-nine, I had only had a few people pass away in my life. But I had always hoped that time would come once you reach an older age, have found the love of your life, raised a family, started wearing hearing aids, and completed crossword puzzles in a recliner.

Death was an uncomfortable conversation for me, and when it came up, I wanted it over before it even began. If it made its way into a discussion, I would promptly and awkwardly change the subject.

When I received the text from Lauren at 3:36 p.m. that Lucas had passed away, my heart dropped. Then my chest hurt and my hands went numb. I had felt these sensations before. Not only was it real this time, it also was final.

Lucas's death was out of the ordinary. He was not an old man. He didn't have years and years under his belt; heck, he hadn't even hit the age of thirty. His mom lost her son. His siblings lost their brother. His wife lost her husband only three years into marriage. All of their lives were flipped upside down.

This was the same Lucas who had survived a catastrophic motorcycle accident where he wasn't supposed to pull through, but he did. After the doctors thought he would never walk again, he was back to running only months later. After his accident, he was prescribed opioids for the pain, and this became the onset of his addiction. Years later, he had a second dance with death. He was in a coma lasting almost three days from a potential overdose. His heart was fluttering, and they didn't know if he would wake up. But he did.

Needless to say, I've felt the roller coaster of helplessness before. You feel unstable. You feel unsure. And you feel sick to your stomach.

That night, I drove home from work, opened a bottle of champagne, and cried while I drafted a letter that was never given to Lucas's wife and is still saved on my laptop. I started to look through countless photos of him, all reminders of some of the best times of my life that he had made a point to be a part of.

The next evening, I taught the 6:30 p.m. yoga class. I closed the hour and a half with *namaste*, stepped off the podium, and left the sweaty yogis in their final *savasana*. I felt lifeless . . . like I was floating in the air and had no weight in my body to keep me on solid ground. I thought that it must have been the most morbid class the students had ever taken.

I stood at the front desk and put a smile on my face to say goodbye to my students as they exited the studio and back into their lives. Ironically, I have *never* had so many students tell me they enjoyed my class and how it was exactly what they needed before they walked out the door that night. No matter how I feel, I am able to channel and give more than what I feel like I have. I hoped happiness still resided somewhere inside me, even when it felt so far removed from my body.

The next day, I took class and went to lunch with my fellow yoga teacher. I ran into an old friend from Costa Mesa there. I had never felt so fake in my life, saying hi and answering his questions: "How are you!? What's new? How's everything going?"

I lied about everything: "I'm good! Nothing new. Everything's great!"

I felt like a walking zombie. I felt dead inside.

As I sat down, not wanting to bring up such a depressing topic, my teacher friend knew what happened and acknowledged the elephant in the room. We had an amazing and life-changing conversation. She told me exactly what I needed to hear. She assured me that "This life is so short compared to the next one that's ahead . . ." and that "part of them is always with you, everywhere you go."

I'll never forget how impactful her words were and how important she was to me at that moment. I was broken, and there was a long road ahead for me to feel normal again.

The Coldest Heart

After crying on and off for six days, I found myself on a flight to Washington. The funeral for Lucas felt surreal, and to this day, I recall it like a terrible dream.

It was held in a church that used to be a grocery store. It was the one my mom used to shop at when I was little and would sit in the grocery cart. She would often grab Skittles or M&M's off the shelf and let me eat them as she shopped. She would then show the clerk the empty bag as our groceries were rung up. It's probably one of the earliest memories I can recall.

Here we were in this same place; the cement walls were dark and bare, and what used to be a grocery store was now a church auditorium. It felt large and lifeless. The heater was on, but there was a permanent chill over my body.

As we went in and sat down, there were endless rows of seats. When I found one about halfway to the stage, I sat down, and the seat provided a more comfortable cushion than I expected: my body melted into the chair. It felt desolate in the room, but people kept filing in. None of us wanted to be there.

I looked down at my hands. I was holding his obituary.

I can read this, and I can feel it with my fingers, but it isn't real for me.

About a minute before the service was to start, his friends all walked in together. Every last one of them, maybe fifteen in total. Once the last one sat down, it felt like the wind was knocked out of me. I had never seen that group of guys without Lucas. Every new event felt like another blow to my reality. Then his family walked in, their heads all hung low. His wife was wearing an oversized red plaid shirt that I recognized had belonged to him.

There were two pastors who spoke at his service. One was a family friend, and the other was my former senior English teacher from high school. This was the same person who wrote on my paper that my story needed to be told when I compared my life to Dante's *Inferno*. The family asked him to speak because while he was a teacher at the high school, he had also been Lucas's baseball coach.

Both of their eulogies felt empty. They didn't do much talking about Lucas or explaining who he was as a person. Their messages were more biblically based around what it means to die and how we should be spending our life here on earth.

I felt uneasy. *What about how he could light up a room by just being in it? What about what a great friend he was? What about how he was an advocate for following your dreams?*

Once they had both finished, his sister got up on stage and walked over to the piano. I admired her bravery. Her fingers moved so gracefully across the black and white keys as she beautifully sang "Lost Boy." It's a song about the story of Peter Pan, the boy from Neverland who chose to never grow up and instead ran away from reality. Lucas never accepted reality, and he would also never get the chance to grow up.

After the service, I walked up to give Lucas's family hugs. His mom squeezed me tight and whispered in my ear, "I knew you would be here. Thank you so much for coming."

I stepped out of the grim auditorium and saw his wife. She was surrounded, and there was a long line of people waiting to give their condolences. As I watched, it appeared as though they would say some words, and she wouldn't respond. I didn't want to intrude on a conversation, but I also didn't want to leave without giving her a hug.

After what felt like countless minutes, I approached her. I wasn't even sure how she would react as we weren't friends, but she had known I was a long-time friend of Lucas.

A little nervous to talk with her, I walked up right as she turned toward me. It looked as though her body started to weaken. She wrapped her arms around me and started sobbing. I, too, began to cry. I held on. And once I started to let go, she continued to hold on. Then countless tears streamed down my face as I held her close. I softly said, "I am so sorry. I love you so much and I loved Lucas. He was the very best guy friend that I could have ever asked for. I know he loved you so, so much—you want to know why? You were the first girlfriend he never talked shit about."

She laughed through her tears and thanked me for coming.

Lauren and I headed out through the church doors and walked to the end of the parking lot, which was completely packed on a Monday. Lauren knew the exact same Lucas that I did. A lot of our memories were made all together. Lucas would ask to join Lauren any time she came down to visit. They had been the two that always put in the most effort to stay connected with me.

Once we arrived at the car, Lauren and I stared blankly at each other. I had no words, but I was okay. It was a lot to take in: a surreal event that I knew would hit me later.

We got in the car and made our way to Overflow Taps. There, I got to talk to more people since the funeral attendees were told to come by after the service.

The place was packed.

While we were there, I saw his best friend, the one who had lived in San Diego. I had hung out with him only a few times, so I didn't know him well. I felt nervous yet compelled to tell him I was sorry for his loss. I gently alerted him by touching his shoulder to talk to him. I envisioned the two of us simply having a short and sad conversation, but I was in utter shock at his words.

My broken heart felt tossed on cement, then trampled on, repeatedly. Not due to any new or additional information, but he was fuming that his best friend died from something that could have been prevented. When he, family, or other friends offered to help Lucas, not only would he ignore their offer, but he would also shut them out until he felt he wanted to be in contact with them again. No one could tell Lucas what to do.

His best friend had no filter for his words. He rambled, and my brain became hazy. It was like rapid fire, one angry comment after another. He was forceful, and rightfully so. His best friend went into cardiac arrest and died after a three-week unassisted attempt to detox himself from drugs.

Then there was the let-up. He ended his harsh words on the only high note that afternoon.

"He loved you," he said. "It was *crazy* how much he loved you. You were a trailblazer. You followed your dreams. You got out of Lynden, and for that, I think he always looked up to you."

My whole intention was to give my condolences, but what I encountered was more than I could handle. While it was good for me to hear what his friend had to say, I couldn't take it. It was all too real. Lucas shouldn't have been so stubborn.

As soon as I could politely make my getaway, I gave the best friend a hug, sidestepped around other groups of people conversing, and made a beeline to the bathroom. I went into the large stall, locked the door, and before I even sat down, tears were flowing down my face.

Later that evening, Lucas's little sister showed up and sat with us. She talked a lot and I didn't say much. I listened to everything she had to say. She was honest, strong, and real.

Before we left for the evening, I gave her a big hug, but when I started to speak, I had a quiver in my voice. With tears in my eyes, I squeezed her tight and whispered in her ear, "You remind me so much of your brother."

Back Home

As my plane took off the next morning from dreary Bellingham, I stared out the window. My eyes focused on the window itself, and I realized that the rain streaming down my little opening into the wet and gloomy world was strikingly similar to the tears that were rolling down my cheeks.

What now? I wondered.

Once we landed back in California, I pulled up my shade and the sun immediately beamed in through my window. I looked to the right, then to the left, and I did not see even one cloud in the sky. I grabbed my notebook to put on paper what came to my mind. After a whirlwind of a trip, I felt in that moment I could explain the realizations circling within me, so I wrote to my friend.

> *Lucas,*
>
> *You were there when I needed someone most. God literally put you into my life for a reason, and I hate that I know that now but didn't see it then. I wish I could tell you how weird it was to see all your friends and not see you. I wish I could tell you how sad, lost, and in disbelief so many of*

> *your friends and family are. You are incredibly missed! So many people will never be the same. As much as this has made me cry every day, I'm going to be strong. Your laugh was contagious, you made me feel so special when you would come to visit every three months, and even in our last texting conversations, you left me laughing. I know you want nothing more than for me to enjoy the sunshine and this life in California, just as you always did when you were still here. I miss you and will continue to miss you every day.*
>
> *Heidi*

The Call

A week or so passed after I arrived back home. I attended a yoga class and felt a hint of rejuvenation inside.

As I was driving home during rush hour, I scrolled through my favorites to call a friend to help take my mind off the stop-and-go traffic. I made my selection and the phone started to ring. It rang and rang, and then the voicemail came: "Hey, it's Lucas. You've . . ."

I quickly hit the red button to end the call. I was taken aback by my obvious mistake. My heart sank. I still wasn't accustomed to him no longer being there for me. He had *always* been there before.

The next month, my yoga studio had a thirty-day challenge where we could attend class as many times in thirty days as possible. Near the end of class, I felt a piercing tightness in my neck and upper back. I tried not to make it noticeable to the other yogis practicing around me in the crowded room during challenge month, but I was suddenly in excruciating pain. I went through the motions for the final posture, took a quick *savasana* at the end of class, and once the teacher said *namaste* and left the room, I immediately followed.

When I went to bed that night, I thought maybe I needed sleep, and it would feel better in the morning. But the next day, I couldn't even sit up. I had to roll myself over and gently push myself up to get out of bed and was still in terrible pain.

I texted one of the other teachers since her husband is a physical therapist. He was able to squeeze me in about an hour before I would pick up Lauren and her husband from the airport for the weekend to celebrate our anniversaries, one year and one day apart.

As he worked on me, he told me my body had tightened up and that he needed to open up areas in my neck, shoulders, and sternum. He talked to me about chronic pain and how some people live this way all the time with little or no relief. My daily posture wasn't helping my situation since I am tall, have long limbs, and my shoulders tend to hunch forward naturally. It took him over an hour to work on my body's resistance.

I told him how thankful I was for him seeing me at the last minute and that I was impressed he knew exactly what the issue was. Obviously, he's a professional and knows what he's doing. But I'll never forget how he responded: "Even though people are different shapes and sizes, some with longer or shorter limbs than others, our bodies are all virtually the same. It's our minds that are different. . . ."

I knew mentally I had closed up, and now my body was trying to follow suit.

The Next Big Thing

One afternoon while waiting for Jude to be off work, I remembered he had told me about some new homes in Chino he passed near his station. I knew the area well: it was off a street I used to take on my route to high school each morning. There was so much new construction that a large housing community now existed where there previously used to be dairyland.

I drove over to walk the models and learned that most of the houses in that area had already been purchased. The agent let me know of another location they were building that was also in Chino, just a few miles away. After returning home that evening, I continued my search online.

In this newer area, there was a community that offered an ideal floor plan, but the model homes hadn't been finished yet, nor had any of the houses been built. I saw their grand opening for the public was scheduled when we would be on vacation with Jude's family. When the day came, my parents went to tour the model I had been eyeing on the website in hopes of potentially putting a deposit down.

I was sitting on the back porch at the house overlooking the lake on our family vacation when my dad called to let me in on what they had learned.

"How is it?" I eagerly asked. I had him on speakerphone so Jude could listen in.

"The floorplan is just like it shows online. Your mom and I were the first ones there. We took a closer look at the lots themselves and determined which ones would face the sunrise. We think lot eight would be the best one."

Then there was silence.

"So . . . should we do it?" I asked.

"Ha!" he replied.

I was looking for someone to make this huge decision for us.

"Well, I think it's exactly what you want. After we were there not even five minutes, they tried to raise the price of your model, but the lady in charge said they would have to honor the price on the original piece of paper she handed us when we walked in," he said.

Jude and I exchanged surprised glances. "Do you want us to sign the check?" my dad asked eagerly.

I looked at Jude.

"Yes. Let's do it!" I replied.

And just like that, we bought a house, sight unseen, in Chino. I was moving back to where my double life began.

17

Chrysalis

I wasn't worried about turning thirty. That was the least of my concerns.

Even though on the exterior one would presume things in my life were working in my favor, I was living under a dark cloud, and I no longer had profound feelings in my life. I would wake up without a smile, which was highly unusual for me, and I couldn't think of a single thing I was looking forward to that week or beyond. Everything felt overwhelming, nothing seemed exciting, and my goals and dreams felt pointless.

When my birthday came around, that same dark cloud reminded me how Lucas never forgot it. After moving to California, even Lauren forgot my birthday entirely one year. We laugh about it now, because it can be an easy oversight and it's not that big of a deal the older we get. However, Lucas and I had been friends for fourteen years at that point, and he had never missed my birthday.

As I headed in to work that Monday, my phone was blowing up with happy birthday messages and voicemails. I received a text from my cousin, who was also named Lucas. It made me smile. He is one of the kindest people I know.

One time when I flew back to Seattle, he picked me up from the airport, drove me to Lynden, and then turned around and headed home. This likely took him almost four hours round trip since Lynden and Seattle are over an hour and a half apart. My cousin Lucas is known for going above and beyond and out of his way to help his family and friends.

Well, see? I told myself, *I did get a happy birthday from Lucas, just not* my *Lucas.*

The day continued. We had recently switched back over to our previous web designer at my dad's business. My dad had known the web designer, ironically also named Lucas, since he was eighteen, and Lucas would complete ad hoc jobs for companies like ours. Lucas and I knew each other since we went to school at the same university, and we would see one another between classes on campus and say hello. My dad and I were on a call with him to discuss the website, and my dad mentioned it was my birthday.

"Aww, happy birthday Heidi!" he said.

"Thanks!" I replied.

All right, that's odd, I thought to myself. *Another Lucas.*

I couldn't help but grin.

With only an hour left at work before leaving for the day, I was talking with a customer on the phone who had questions about his recent order. After a rather lengthy conversation, I told him, "I sincerely apologize, but I actually have to leave here in just a few minutes. But feel free to send me an email if you need anything further."

"Oh, is this the time you normally close?" he asked. "I'm curious in case I need to call back later this week with a question."

Caught off guard, I replied, "Well, no . . . it's actually my birthday today, so I'm leaving a bit earlier than normal."

"Oh! Well, no problem, I'll send an email if I need anything further. And happy birthday!" he exclaimed.

"Thank you!" I responded, a little embarrassed. "I'm sorry, but I don't think I got your name."

"My name is Lucas."

Tears instantly welled up in my eyes and rolled down my face. It may sound silly, but I felt an overwhelming calm. In a roundabout way, I received my "Happy Birthday" from Lucas. It felt like he was there, telling me through those three people that day.

Maybe he didn't miss my birthday after all.

One Foot in Front of the Other

Jude and I moved out of our apartment and were living as vagabonds between his parents, my parents, and my sister's place in Huntington Beach. I had a lot of vacations scheduled before the end of the year: Cabo for a family trip, San Francisco for a wedding, a last-minute cheap flight to see the Tinky Winkies, and then Chicago for my middle sister's wedding. Our house was scheduled to be completed just days before the end of the year.

During the next two months, there were three other losses of people I was connected to: my friend's mom, another friend's brother, and my other friend's two-week-old baby. My anxiety peaked and I felt as though my emotions could easily shift from one moment to the next at the drop of a hat from happy to depressed. I didn't have an answer for Lucas's death, and I sure had no answers for these devastating losses either.

When I would wake up in the morning, a tightness would start in my chest, and I couldn't get rid of it as the day passed. I felt heavy in my day-to-day life. I couldn't talk to anyone about it, nor did I want to. I attempted to keep my depressing and negative outlook on life under wraps. On one of my saddest days, when I was contemplating what the point of life was, one of my closest friends asked me, "Do you wake up positive? How are you so happy all the time?"

Wow. I've gotten really good at putting on a smile with a gaping hole in my heart. But hadn't I done this my whole life? Things can always appear put together on the outside, but something was off inside of me. It was the most out of sync I had ever been.

Looking back, I should have gone to therapy. I rehearsed in my head how I would ask Jude to agree for me to go, but I didn't want him to think I was unhappy with *him*. He was what brought me the most joy during that time. He was my person, but he wasn't the one to solve my sadness.

While so many wonderful things were happening, the huge losses had a tight hold on my heart. My chest hurt, my body was closing up, and I felt as though I was spinning into a chrysalis. All I wanted was out.

I've learned that metamorphosis is an amazing process. When it begins, a caterpillar hardens its outer layer to become a chrysalis. While that looks calm and steady from the outside, on the inside a crazy yet magical change is taking place. In just days, the inside of the caterpillar melts into a pile of goo, and its body breaks down before its insides are reorganized into the structures that allow it to emerge as a butterfly. The caterpillar transforms its old messy state into something new and exquisite. Everything the caterpillar needed to become a butterfly was inside it from day one. The caterpillar didn't require something it didn't already have. I didn't want to be wrapped up in sadness or grief any longer. But in order for that to be the case, a massive shift or complete transformation needed to happen within me.

A girl in our extended friend group is a therapist. Once our schedules aligned, I talked her through my condensed list of notes from my own introspection of what I recognized as my core issues. It was the most honest I had been to anyone about myself.

I told her how I thought I was an empath because I deeply take on the emotions of others. I also told her that I thought I was a highly sensitive person (HSP). People who are HSP are often affected by positive or negative situations in life and feel easily overwhelmed from different triggers.[1]

Since I can remember, I take comments others make personally and ruminate on people's words or opinions endlessly. I habitually clutch onto the negative parts, similar to how one would relentlessly hold onto a life preserver in a dire time of need in the middle of the open ocean. There was no means of me letting go of these preconceived notions in the foreseeable future. I was my own biggest critic. I avoided my true feelings and created an overly cheerful exterior in the process that would have people certain I was happy through and through.

After a few hours of discussion with her, me speaking my truth and hearing how she battled anxiety herself, I felt normal, understood, and not alone. It was the step I needed to move forward. My deep wounds had to be opened up and exposed in order for them to heal.

The next month, I woke up one morning to a dozen texts from a friend saying that there had been a shooting at the Route 91 Harvest Festival in Las Vegas . . . and that she was there! She was scared, she said, but okay. My hands started to shake uncontrollably. Everything in life continued to feel fragile, and it was all out of my control.

I can't take anything more going wrong. It's too much.

That evening, I attended church in Chino with my cousin. It was close to where Jude and I would be moving in a matter of months. The service began with an announcement that they were providing counselors and other resources for anyone who either attended the concert or needed help. They did not have specialized counselors on staff, so they asked for donations from the congregation to assist in paying for those services. It moved me. I had attended church my entire life and couldn't recall a time they dropped everything and provided support during such a devastating time of need.

Once we moved to our new house in Chino, we became members at that same church. Within two weeks of attending, the head pastor gave a sermon that changed the trajectory of my sad state. Tears fell down my cheeks as I wrote down his three main points and listened to his words: *When God Says No—The Greatest Test of Faith: (1) When He has a bigger perspective, (2) a better plan, or (3) a greater purpose.*

I took some additional notes that said: *Some things won't make sense until Heaven. Some problems won't change until Heaven. Some suffering is for the benefit of others.* Previously, to cope with Lucas's death, I practiced yoga, meditation, and breathwork. I also cleared my schedule and started talking openly about my sadness with friends. I started to feel better, but I couldn't kick the sick feeling in the pit of my stomach or escape the dark cloud that followed me everywhere I went. But after hearing his sermon, it was only then that I experienced an overwhelming peace for the first time since losing Lucas.

Life can be messy and unpredictable, but God has the greatest viewpoint of not just my life but all our lives and the world as a whole. I've learned that being a Christian doesn't mean there's a lack of struggles; rather, it gives us the Truth to cling to when troubles inevitably come.

The Realization

As the end of summer was approaching, the Tinky Winkies had a trip planned to visit. I was excited to be with the girls and felt I could really use some bonding time with them. Erika and I had previously chatted on the phone where we both apologized for what happened that weekend at the lake. Over the last four years, we hadn't stayed super connected. I had a year of teaching as much as I could with no trips to Washington, then we had Lauren's wedding events as well as mine. She flew in for my bachelorette weekend and then my wedding, which was the last time I saw her.

She made a point to be a part of the big stuff. So while things between us felt the same, they were also totally different. Although our lives and friendship took a massive shift, I love her just as much as I did back when we were teenagers swapping bathing suits on the waterslide or taking long bike rides to meet our boyfriends, and I always will.

I picked the girls up from the airport in Orange County, and we went down to Newport Beach to grab lunch. As we sat down at our table, I noticed a mantraband on my friend's wrist. I had a few of these bracelets, including one that said *Namaste* and another that reminded me, *The Best Is Yet to Come.*

"Oh! I love those," I said, reaching for her wrist. "What does yours say?"

I spun the band around and read the word *Soulmates.*

"Oh!" I continued. "That's so sweet. Who do you have it with?"

That's when the moment got awkward.

I turned my head to see another friend across the table from me place her hand over her wrist to hide her bracelet and lower her arm beneath the table. It turned out they all had the same band. All of them except me.

I told myself, *It's not a big deal, it's not a big deal.*

But it hurt. Did I miss *our* episode of *Survivor*? The one where I was collectively voted off the island and out of the group?

It came at a strange time for me, or maybe it was the *right* time. I was in the middle of feeling a part of everything but not really a part of anything. I lived too far away to still be included in the Tinky Winkies. Then I moved inland and wasn't hanging out with my "sweat sisters," a.k.a. my yoga teacher friends, on the regular or seeing them at the studio multiple days a week. Meanwhile, Chloe lived in NorCal, so the group of girls that included her and Ella was a little dispersed as well. I felt alone on my island of Chino.

But during my weekend with the Tinky Winkies, I chose to forget about the bracelet and enjoyed my time with them. We caught up on work, life, husbands and boyfriends, and kids (or plans to start trying for them). After our beach day, we spent two days lying on floaties at the pool, sipping on sweet beverages and working on our tans. It's amazing how much had happened since we were initially formed back in the sixth grade, yet we continued to have our strong bond. Our inside jokes still felt unmatched.

As the girls were lining up their suitcases at the front door getting ready to catch their flight back home, my Tinky Winky friend handed me her *Soulmates* bracelet.

"Oh, it's fine. It's yours. I don't need it," I said confidently.

"Yes, you do," she urged. "It's now yours."

I sighed.

"Thank you." I replied.

I was sad to see them go. They are some of the biggest contributors to who I am today. These girls had been my lifeline. While life took us in different directions and kept us living in separate locations, I know they will always have a special place in my heart. To this day, no amount of time all together ever feels like enough.

Inner Child

After attending a Bikram yoga class, I showered and stayed after for one of my favorite teacher's hour-long meditation classes. While practicing meditation was an entirely new world I had explored largely due to the sadness in my life, I received a lot of advice that it was imperative to calming my anxiety.

My amazing teacher, someone I consider to be a present-day guru, is the only person I have met in life that I would consider to be "self-realized." His calm method of teaching is how I aspire to be when I teach a yoga class.

To begin, we were standing in a circle, swinging our arms around, then shaking our hands and getting the wiggles out. It helped us to release energy and enabled us to sit still for the next hour or more. About three-quarters of the way into our practice, after a prolonged silence sitting in our stillness, he prompted us with: "Imagine your five-year-old self. What would you tell that little person today?"

While I had previously attended only a few of his meditations, this one sparked something in me. I pictured myself back when I was five. I had light blonde hair with loose curls. I was entering kindergarten at my small-town private school. I was happy then, and I knew I was ultimately happy now. It just took me some time to get back there.

Without warning, the tears came. I didn't have to think about it. I knew exactly what I would tell my five-year-old self.

I would say, "Do not worry. Your life is going to work out better than you could ever imagine."

That was part of my problem all along: not knowing, feeling torn, replaying the lie in my head that I was a bad kid, and constantly questioning my direction in life. But here I was, happily married and working my dream job. I had friends and family who loved and supported me, and while I abruptly lost my friend, I knew it was part of the duality of life. I was on my way to healing, and I was certain everything was going to be okay.

I learned that exposing your vulnerability, rawness, and sadness is what will help to open you up and heal faster. The longer those emotions stay compressed inside of you, the less control you will have over them when they finally escape. I was thankful to have jobs where I could get in a hot room and sweat it out or go into work with my hair in a messy bun and no makeup. I needed the time and space to crack and tear myself apart before mending and rebuilding the new me. All this time, these troubles, or things that came my way which I thought were to break me, were actually necessary for my breakthrough.

Ultimately, I knew in my heart that Lucas had always been one of my biggest supporters and was happy for my happiness. He flew down to say goodbye before I left to study abroad and then visited again to watch me give the commencement speech on graduation day. He was always there to not only celebrate my big accomplishments but also to celebrate me. When I release this book and pop a bottle of champagne for a toast, I know he will be there in spirit.

It wasn't until he lost his life that I realized all he had given me. He gave me something to hold onto and something to look forward to. It's wild to see now, in hindsight, how he was there for me when I absolutely needed someone most. I have peace knowing that with a small glimpse of his life from my point of view captured in this book will help the Lucas I knew to never die.

Stepping Stones

As I processed grief and overcame struggles with my mental health, there were several coping strategies that helped me move past the pain.

How I Overcame Grief, Depression, and Reduced My Anxiety

1. Crying for two weeks straight: let it out, don't keep it in
2. Talking to my friends that knew the friend I lost; staying in touch with his family
3. Knowing I would never "get over it" and instead accepting to live with it
4. Talking out loud in the car and recording myself explaining how I felt
5. Listening to meditations: specifically releasing, "The past which is unchangeable and the future which is yet to occur" and sitting with my emotions in the present moment
6. Reducing alcohol intake as a means to simply numb the pain
7. Keeping his picture on my bulletin board—thinking about him every day
8. Knowing he would want me to follow my dreams
9. Letting go of *my* plan and letting God's will happen
10. Keeping in perspective that this life is short—the next life is forever
11. Reviewing my pastor's sermon notes, "When God Says No"

12. Sitting with the grief; giving myself time; making a point of self-care
13. Keeping busy (that's how I handle things), then slowing down and creating space; finding balance in my routine
14. Knowing when to ask for help
15. Getting enough exercise and sleep
16. Eating healthy
17. Learning to say no; creating boundaries
18. Praying and reading scripture
19. Noticing and changing my thoughts: *Where's your focus? What's your perspective?*
20. Real-life conversations: spending time with Jude, time with my friends, less time on my phone

Part 6

Happiness is a butterfly, which when pursued,
is always beyond your grasp, but which,
if you will sit down quietly, may alight upon you.

—Nathaniel Hawthorne

18

Butterfly

It was fitting how my transformation and the huge shift in my mind happened right as I felt a chill in the air that fall. The leaves were turning, displaying vibrant colors before the trees would shed them to the ground and bare their limbs. Changes were apparent all around me, but, most importantly, they were happening inside of me.

Late September is when I woke up feeling different. I felt awake and eager for what was to come. Although Jude was gone for a seven-week-long training for a promotional position, as each day passed, we were that much closer to him returning home for the rest of the year.

Those seven weeks gave me the space I needed to put myself first. The old me would have filled my time with every unnecessary thing, but now I believe those blank squares rarely on my calendar are the moments where life is inviting me to rest and decompress.

I calmed my stress and anxiety by tending to my mind, body, and soul. I went to bed early, caught up with close friends, listened to meditations weekly, cleansed my body of toxins, worked out five to six times each week, and went to church every Sunday. I sat with my emotions, and I allowed myself to cry when I felt sad. It was the first time I had ever slowed down the merry-go-round of my life.

Since I can remember, I desired control over how my life would unfold, yet I have learned it will develop exactly how it is meant to. All I can control is me: what I think about, how I spend my time, how I respond to people, whom I keep in my life, and how I react to situations.

So, I thought to myself, *that had been my problem all along: I simply needed to change my mind.*

I finally went to therapy. I wanted to reassure myself that my own shadow work had not been in vain and that there wasn't something deeper wrong with me. I also wanted to confirm that all the self-reflection I had done was in fact the truth about myself. While I know everyone in this human experience struggles with something, I knew I had it good, and there are so many others who have worse trauma in their life. But when I mentioned this to my therapist, she responded to me saying this: "It doesn't matter if you're drowning in the ocean, a pool, or a puddle, the sensation feels the same."

She was right. I had been drowning in my negative thinking for years. I had worked on the relationship with myself but always allowed the setbacks to keep me from growing or being completely happy.

But the beautiful thing about shadows is it means that there is light emitted somewhere: you're not completely in darkness, even if there is an obstacle between you and the light. I hadn't been completely in the dark this whole time, but I had chosen to stay in those shadows. I simply needed to step into the light.

I wanted to make right in my mind what never felt right in my soul. I stopped fighting myself to understand it: moving to Chino in the middle of senior year, finding Jude, losing my friend Lucas, the good and the bad, the ups and the downs—it was all a part of it. It *had* to be. You don't fully appreciate the sunshine if you haven't felt the rain. You can't comprehend the magic of a best friend unless you've encountered selfish ones. You may not value true love unless you've overcome a broken heart. And you can't imagine what a treasure it is to release unwanted anxiety after conquering sadness and deep grief through choosing to embrace life's unpredictable but beautiful path.

I attended a workshop and those few sessions of therapy within weeks of one another, and both communicated a similar message: we all have core beliefs about ourselves that we likely established in our early years of life. Some of mine were (1) I'm a great friend, and (2) I'm good at volleyball. After the move during my senior year, I added (3) I'm a bad kid, and (4) I'm not good enough. We develop narratives along the way that simply aren't true, but like any behavior, we start to believe it, and it has the ability to warp our perception of ourselves. Often we allow it to latch on and become a part of us.

These beliefs we have about ourselves are like pathways in our brain where we run the same thoughts through our minds over and over again. It's up to us to do the work to change them if they're negatively impacting our life.

It wasn't until starting yoga and being aware of my negative thoughts that I even attempted to shift the way I viewed myself from long ago. Instead of traveling along those same pathways,

I made new trails: (1) I am creating the life of my dreams, and (2) I deserve to be happy.

Previously, I attempted to perfectly position my surroundings in life to solve the agitation I felt inside. I worked hard to align my goals to create fulfillment in my heart: being a big sister, leaving public accounting, meeting the love of my life, becoming a yoga teacher, and getting married. But the answer wasn't a profitable career, the right guy, or the location I lived. Those external circumstances would not be my solution to my internal conflict.

Social media doesn't do us any favors either: It has allowed us to believe that everyone is thriving based on their feeds, making us think we must be the outliers in our struggles. It creates a sense of comparison that doesn't tell the whole story of what's really going on behind the lens.

I was guilty of spending too much time on how my life was perceived by others. I also felt that with the life I lived, I shouldn't be ungrateful for all that I had. I worried about or tried to control each and every moment of my experience, thereby counteracting the nature of life itself. This created my perpetual disappointment. I lived a calculated life, hoping it would go exactly how I envisioned it should. After years of my continuous resistance, I needed to surrender to forces far greater than myself: the duality of life and His divine timing.

Losing Lucas was the final straw that sparked my existential crisis or my "dark night of the soul" encounter.[1] There is usually an event, one unpredictable and oftentimes tragic, that can turn your life upside down. This was what I was in the thick of for almost a year after losing him. The flip side of this, however, is that once you navigate through it, it can allow you to be rebirthed or opened up to your deeper sense of meaning.

The Result

Once Jude was back from his training, the holidays hit, and my life was coming together like never before. With Jude home, everything felt back to normal and right on track. We agreed to start trying to have a family. My heart was at peace, and I felt excited for the future.

I took a pregnancy test on New Year's Eve. It was instantly negative. Three days later, Jude went golfing with his best friend and sent me a text asking if I had taken another test. It was unlike me to avoid it, but I believed the results of the one I had already taken.

But listening to his suggestion, I took two more tests that morning and sent Jude the results. They were both inconclusive: the control line was not there, but the pregnant line was solid blue. When this happens, the instructions deem the test to be invalid.

Jude showed his friend the photo of the tests I had sent him. His friend, who already had two kids of his own, told Jude, "Looks like she's pregnant to me!"

Later that day, we purchased a digital test to give us a straight answer: YES or NO. This time, Jude came into the bathroom with me and joked, "I'm here to monitor and ensure that you properly execute the task at hand."

Irritated, I replied, "I know how to pee on a stick!"

I didn't like the anticipation I felt, so I stepped out of the bathroom while the result was loading. I felt the entire day had been built up to make me think I actually *was* pregnant and what a letdown it would be when I found out I wasn't.

Jude was eager to see the result and stayed in the bathroom, watching it load. Not even ten seconds later, a booming voice shouted, "We're pregnant!"

While that dark cloud had previously hung above me, it all dissipated when I entered my second trimester, coinciding with my nausea subsiding. I began to wrap my mind around entering into motherhood. You could say I was finally pushing my way out of the chrysalis, spreading my wings, and transforming into a butterfly.

Ironically, at that same time, swarms of butterflies were fluttering all over Southern California. The month of March in 2019 set records for the monarch migration schedule. This species of butterfly is known to navigate the furthest and endure the most strenuous journey. The swarms I observed were the result of an unusually heavy migration making their way from Mexico to Canada to breed, according to the experts.[2] Butterflies were everywhere. The coincidence was heavenly. It felt magical. It felt meant for me.

A few weeks later, I went to lifeguard tower 36 before sunrise one morning. This was the tower that had been in direct proximity to my condo when I lived in Newport Beach and started my big-girl job.

Sitting there, I wrote in my journal what I was grateful for: the day off, a wonderful husband, a baby on the way, a beautiful home, the ability to pursue my dreams, amazing memories, a small group at my new church that I instantly connected with, my parents' excitement about becoming grandparents, my yoga community, girlfriends who supported me near and far, God's grace, and a clearer vision for my life.

Clouds surrounded the sun as it came up that morning. This cast obvious shadows while distinct beams of light shone through onto the ocean water. It was peaceful and gorgeous. I thought my life would be put together when I moved to these numbered streets in Newport Beach ten years ago, living only ninety-six steps from the sand. I remember thinking to myself, *How could life get better than this?* It appeared glamorous, even though the emptiness on the inside grew. And yet, life got so much better. All of what I thought were wrong turns, detours, and roadblocks were what brought me here.

A Gift

When my daughter turned one, my "silver lining" and lifelong friend I made from my first college gifted her a puzzle of her name and then handed me a small box. I opened the box to find a gold necklace with a large circle emblem paired with a smaller circle. The larger circle had a symbol of a lotus flower, and the smaller circle had a peony.

I was surprised. I had always loved the lotus flower, an icon I often associated with yoga. It's a symbol of self-realization, growth, rebirth, and spiritual enlightenment. I had seen them on display at one of my yoga studios. After doing my research on the flower years ago, I decided I wasn't at a point in my life where I was ready to wear a symbol with such a powerful meaning.

"This is beautiful," I said. "But it's not *my* birthday! You didn't have to get me such a wonderful gift! What's the smaller flower in the circle for?"

"Yes, I did," she replied. "You did a full year as a mom, and you did an amazing job! The circles are the birth flowers for you and your daughter. The month of July is a lotus and September is a peony."

Of course it is.

And it was given to me at the perfect time.

Shifting toward inner peace can be a process of ripping your heart open and exposing its contents. Some refer to it as "shadow work," as it is a process where you embrace the dark parts of you. I've found this to be imperative when it comes to self-awareness and a deeper understanding of yourself, which often is a direct reflection of your journey in life. I am certain peace is not something to be achieved; rather, it is a daily practice to be maintained. But the best way I can give guidance to help others in their endeavor is what I learned through my own process.

Steps to Help Achieve Inner Peace

1. **MIND**: *Release*
    a. Don't try to control every element of how life should be. It will unfold exactly how it is intended to.
    b. Choose to fully live your life. Let go of others' expectations. Set boundaries.
    c. Don't dwell in the past—failed dreams, grief, and loss. Feel the feelings, then let them go.

2. **BODY**: *Align*
    a. Take care of your body and mind—rest and detox.
    b. Do what keeps you feeling alive—fill your cup.
    c. Surround yourself with people who love you and lift you up.
3. **SOUL**: *Love*
    a. Treat yourself as you would your own best friend.
    b. Your thoughts create your reality, which creates your life. Stop the negativity toward yourself. When you focus on the good, the good comes into focus.
    c. Practice gratitude, daily affirmations, read scripture, meditate, and give yourself grace.

Part 7

Miracles start to happen when you give
as much energy to your dreams as you do to your fears.

—Richard Wilkins

19

Full Circle

The ironies and synchronicities continued to connect. Maybe it was obvious for an outsider looking in, but to me, it finally felt like this wild ride I was on finally made sense. It was how my life was always intended to be. The path I took, what I thought was this messy and unpredictable route, was in actuality the trail that led to the essence of me. It included many detours, twists and turns, wrong ways, and seemingly dead ends, but they all brought me to right here.

We had a small family get-together for my daughter's first birthday. Five days before her party, I went in for a prenatal appointment after having a surprise positive pregnancy test. I started bleeding the day before, so I went in with the belief that something must be wrong.

There was no heartbeat.

During the family celebration, I felt completely torn in two: equally grateful for my firstborn to turn one year old and simultaneously mourning the loss of one who would have been her sibling. It's one of those circumstances you never want to be in. On the exterior, I held it together, but I would often cry in the car or in the closet by myself while she would nap. It caught me completely off guard and felt like an inexplicable loss.

A few months later, my dad told me that there was a new Vinyasa yoga studio being built a few miles from my house. Since I was certified specifically in Bikram, I wasn't contemplating teaching there but thought I would check it out once it opened. I decided to satisfy my own curiosity and looked it up online. The studio offered six different types of yoga classes; one of them was hot yoga. I watched the demo video on my computer and saw a lot of postures that crossed over to the Bikram series.

I could teach that!

So I applied on a whim, made a demo video of myself teaching a Vinyasa flow for the very first time, got the job, and taught the first class upon the studio's opening on April 17, the same day that would have been my due date.

Teaching there, I am continually reminded of the sentiment that even in the midst of sad things, new and wonderful things can still emerge from the broken pieces. With every ending comes a new beginning. This doesn't mean I wasn't sad or I easily moved on. I am not immune to deeply feeling tough times or disappointing moments or circumstances, but I choose to embrace and accept any unforeseen turn of events with a completely different mindset than before. I've learned that even the biggest losses can reveal unexpected silver linings.

The Signs

Months later, after my son was born, it was summertime and we started taking trips to the river. We stayed at the same river house with the dock where Chloe and I talked about burnt pizza and Jude and I discussed our future wedding. Today, it is where I create memories with my kids.

On our most recent trip, I had a moment when I gazed up at my two children standing on the dock, each in their puffy and a bit oversized life vests paired with water shoes, both making the same face, squinting their bright blue eyes hidden behind their little kid shades in the Arizona sun. I gazed at my daughter's blonde ponytail and my son with his wild curly hair, and my moment of taking in the present while reminiscing the past was broken with "Mom! Will you go in the water with me?" While I imagined a lot of dreams for my life, these small moments hit differently.

I find myself thinking about my children's journeys and what their big purposes will be in this world. It took me until my thirties to understand my life and the reason for the crazy ride, and it would be wonderful for my kids to learn from my mistakes and take the shortcut to where I am now: accepting life's highs and lows, sitting with feelings, loving myself through it, and knowing that everything will work out exactly how it is intended to.

Being a mom has reiterated my need to release the lack of control I have every day. My to-do list often takes a backseat to riding my toddler's emotional roller coaster, and I can choose for it to end by offering a much-needed hug instead of sending him or her to their room.

While I attempted to prepare myself mentally for slowing down my life and staying home far more often than ever before, I wasn't ready for the daily tasks, messy house, tantrums, calming the tantrum within myself, and trying to reason with completely unreasonable tiny humans. The lack of a carefree mentality was more challenging than I thought it could ever be. I'm in "Mom mode" from the moment I wake up until bedtime and even in the middle of the night.

But I am reminded daily that my children reflect me. My daughter copies what I wear, what I say, and what I do, be it brushing our teeth together, washing the dishes, or writing on the calendar. In fact, she asks for a calendar of her own to write on. She likes to set her clothes out for the next morning just as I do and asks to wear my outfits, saying, "Mama, I want to look just like you." My daughter often chooses to run around in a frilly bathing suit or tutu just like I did as a small child.

My son shows similar tendencies: he asks to stir my creamer in my coffee each morning, helps me put away clean clothes, and imitates my yoga postures while I'm crafting a new sequence for class.

They mimic my routine, use my words, and also look up to me as if I'm the greatest person in this world. It makes me stop and evaluate my choices when I realize I want to be everything these tiny people think I am. Maybe my journey molded me to be the best mother possible for them, giving me the intuition necessary to effectively guide them on their individual paths.

My children make me more resilient since the practice of my own peace feels tested every day. I went from an anxious, empathetic high school girl to a mother of two and a firefighter's wife with a crazy schedule. I am no longer a "people-pleaser" since I've learned how to set boundaries, and I choose to trust the process and acknowledge that often people's actions are a reflection of them and not of me. It's taken many hours in the hot room, multiple discussions with wise friends, prayer, and a shift in my thoughts, but it is humbling to see the change in me. I'm growing, they're learning, and I've never loved two little people so much in my life.

After becoming a mom, with the concurrent changes, I would find myself thinking, *This isn't me.* Yet maybe it is! I was transforming into the version of "me" I was always meant to be. And I am certain that being their mom is the most important role I will ever have in my life.

As summer continued, we endured some super-hot days. Summers in SoCal can start as early as April and last all the way to November. Along came a toasty one that June, on the day that would have been Lucas's thirty-fourth birthday. It had been five years since his passing.

I was home with the kiddos that day, and he was obviously on my mind. I missed his idiotic laugh, his daredevil zest for life, and how he rooted me on, but he didn't feel too far away from me that day for some reason.

To take a break from inside activities, we took a walk to the mailbox. Right away, we saw a butterfly, which stopped the kids in their tracks as if they were in a trance. My daughter, completely enthralled, reached out to try and touch it with her finger.

"No thank you, honey. We look with our eyes, not our hands!" I said, gently admonishing her.

As we walked, the butterfly came with us. The next thing I knew, we had passed three houses, crossed the street, and were standing in front of our mailbox, with the butterfly fluttering next to us the entire way.

I started to tear up.

I cannot say why the butterfly followed us, but it felt exceptional. It was almost as if Lucas was with us on our excursion to the mailbox that day.

Next, we took a family trip to San Diego. It's not only where the magic seemed to reside for me, but it was also the place where my dreams came to fruition when Jude proposed.

During our trip, I saw the quote "I am exactly where I am meant to be" randomly painted on a wall in the courtyard where guests could sit and eat their dinner outside. Undoubtedly, it made me smile, as it's exactly how I had been feeling at this point in my life.

I saw that same quote again the next month on my return flight home from Chloe's bachelorette party on a billboard at the airport.

When I read the words, it made me feel startled and caught off guard once again. It felt like it was reiterating that my once torn-apart life had not only been pieced back together but also mended in the best way possible. It was all coming full circle. I wondered, *Was this just now showing up in my life or was I finally noticing it?* Regardless, I couldn't help but feel aligned.

Years back, when I started attending Pacific Academy during my senior year of high school, my world was crushed. But today, my daughter attends that same school. When I take her in the mornings, I often opt for a shortcut which takes us past the dairy farms. I see the black and white cows eating in their fields next to palm trees every time, and it never fails to remind me of that time in my life. When I walked into Pacific Academy on my first day at my new school, I had no thoughts that my future would have a happy ending and that someday my kids would attend school there just as I did.

On Sunday mornings, we often meet my parents after church at a nearby coffee shop. Once there, we order our iced coffees and cake pops for the kids. My daughter insists on touching the rushing water in the fountain while my son runs around looking for bugs. It's the exact Starbucks I sat at with my parents my first Christmas in California almost twenty years ago.

The Road Not Taken

I knew that at some point in my life, Zach would resurface, and we would cross paths. But what are the odds my husband and the only other guy I ever loved would both take part in a hobby like racing Ironmans? This small niche of endurance athletes has only a few races that occur in our corner of the United States each year, making the likelihood of the two of them participating in the same race extremely high.

After learning they would be competing in the same event in the spring, I felt a bit on edge imagining that we would bump into each other. I didn't want to be caught off guard not knowing what to say, a rarity for me. I admittedly wanted control of whenever that awkward moment would happen.

While I wrangled two children and waited for Jude to pass by us, I saw Zach coming our way. "Go, Zach Zimmerman!" I cheered. Without flinching, he kept his game face on along with his quick pace as he flew past us.

The kids and I moved closer to where the finish line was. Being that the race was in Oceanside, the kids played in the sand as we waited. While wading in the water, I ran into Zach's mom, dad, and child. His parents each gave me a hug, as I hadn't seen them in years.

After the race was over, the kids and I found Jude, and we walked with him to the transition area to retrieve his bicycle after his race. I heard someone yell, "Your kids are really cute!"

It was Zach walking toward us.

Jude approached him and shook his hand. They talked Ironman for a few minutes. Finally, Zach turned to me and grinned. "I knew someone who *really* knew me was cheering me on," he said. "Nobody says my first *and* last name like they did back in high school."

It was undoubtedly a weird and full circle moment: a friendly exchange with what felt like a complete stranger.

20

The Best Is Yet to Come

My husband and I invited an elderly friend over one evening for dinner and to give a tour of our new home in Chino. At the time, we had sheets covering the windows while we waited for our shutters to be custom made and installed, a borrowed fridge (since ours was on backorder), and furniture that took up little space in our family room. We chose not to go furniture shopping yet since our down payment on our newly built house took a hit on our bank account.

The interior was spacious, white, and was the beginning of something beautiful while still a work in progress. The majority of our walls were still empty, except for the main wall in the family room. I twisted Jude's arm to hang some décor a couple days after we moved in. I wanted to start putting things in their place to begin transforming this house into our home.

We gave her a tour of our house, and when climbing to the second floor, she needed to stop and catch her breath as she slowly maneuvered up and down our single flight of stairs. At the time, ninety-one years young, she was still out and about with all of her wit.

After the short tour of our home, we retreated downstairs where she sat on the seat of her walker as she listened to the television. We were watching *Wheel of Fortune.*

During the lull of a commercial break, she looked over at our wall, decorated with plaques and photos, and read one of my favorite hangings out loud: "*The Best Is Yet to Come*. Well, ain't that the truth?!"

With a huge smile on my face, since I had planned for the phrase to be the title of my book someday, I replied lovingly, "Yeah! I love it, too!"

As the show came back on and we watched the final round, I couldn't help but be intrigued by her comment. Full disclosure: this woman had won the lottery. No, that's not a figure of speech. She won millions of dollars back in the '90s. This lady also married the love of her life (who had since passed away), has five children, four grandchildren, and five great-grandchildren; donates her money constantly; and enjoys red wine, scratchers, and playing bingo as often as she can. She lives life to the absolute fullest and is the luckiest woman I have ever met.

How at this point could she agree with the phrase on my wall stating The Best Is Yet to Come? *Hadn't her "best" already been?*

During her time spent on this earth, I think she understood the message behind the phrase. We shouldn't view the "best" as memories or those big events in our past for exactly that reason: They're over, and we can't travel back in time to those moments. We can reminisce about the good times that we hold on to or talk about the people who impacted us that are no longer with us, but to say the past was the best would be dreadful, to be honest. Our past is the only thing that can no longer be revisited or changed. There's no longer any life in the past, aside from the memories that reside in our hearts and minds. Life is not only ahead of us in the future but also right in *front* of us each and every moment.

Additionally, the "best" may not necessarily be something in our lifetime or even in time form. Your greatest contribution to life and the whole reason you are here

- could be your legacy
- could be your donations
- could be the children you molded and raised
- could be your children's children
- could be in your last breath knowing you lived a full life

But likely, and even more importantly, it could be the day we rendezvous in Heaven with the people we love most. What a blessing it is to know that *you* have the power to do big things and that *you* aren't finished yet. It is up to you whether or not you allow your goals to be sought after, your dreams to come true, and the fullest version of yourself to emerge. We have the future on our side, giving us the opportunity to change everything.

Connecting the Dots

In my story, there were leading lights along my way; it just took me a while to accept the trail I was guided down. There were moments I contemplated what would have happened had I never been uprooted from my hometown. Would I still have met and married Jude? But just as I crossed paths with my friend studying abroad after visiting her high school to potentially enroll, I firmly believe what is meant to happen absolutely will, no matter the route or trail traveled to arrive at the destination. You cannot mess up what is meant for you.

After being a mom for just a few short years now, I've better understood why my parents were strict with me. They love me. Kids can be crazy, and we experience a lack of control when it comes to their emotions and actions. My parents were doing the best they could to help guide me to make the best decisions for myself. My sisters were also always great examples for me. They are ambitious individuals, encouraged me to study and travel abroad in order to expand my horizons, and were always there when I needed advice.

While my move to Southern California broke my teenage heart, it allowed my world to grow. It pushed me out of the comfort zone of my small town and permitted me to gain even more life experiences. I had a familiar face, my former teacher, help soften the blow that first day at my new school. Even though I felt alone in my new surroundings, I never truly was. At the time, all that I could focus on was what I lost, while simultaneously I gained so many new and wonderful relationships. My move rocked my world, yet it ended up being one of the biggest gifts I'll ever receive. It propelled my life into so much fullness and newness. Today, I live in Chino: the place where, at one point in my life, it broke my heart. But now, living back in this same place, I have become whole.

Studying abroad in Spain gave me confidence that I had the ability to live the life I wanted, wherever I wanted to. My career in public accounting prepared and developed me professionally.

While working at my corporate job, I earned the paid time off to experience all the fun while saving money to pay for my yoga teacher training. Living like *Friends* gave me a supportive "family" during my biggest heartbreak and kept me focused on all that was good in my life instead of what I was in the process of letting go.

Becoming a yoga teacher gave me fulfillment as I encourage and guide others to achieve their goals and dreams. My yoga practice still contributes to lowering my anxiety and continues to connect my mind, body, and soul. Often when I meet others and they learn I am an instructor, their first question is frequently, "If I practice yoga, is it going to change my life?"

The question always makes me smile. Although *my* life significantly changed, it really depends on the person if they will experience any kind of shift or not. The key factor of fostering this growth, whether through yoga or something else, is if the practitioner is open to change or looking for it.

On your trail, I hope you have an Erika: someone who you enjoyed mindless and carefree shenanigans with as a young child. Someone who always cared for you and is the person who continues to cheer you on through all the seasons of your life. And even though life may spread you a little thin, a friend like Erika loves you and *always* shows up for the big stuff.

I hope you have a Lauren, your most dependable friend, no matter when you call, what advice you need, or how many years or miles come in between the two of you, they stand the test of time. They will always be your go-to person. They understand your heart before you even open your mouth to explain a thing.

I hope you have a solid friend group: one you can confide in, be yourself, and create lasting memories with. And even though life takes you in different directions, you magically stay connected. My irreplaceable group, the Tinky Winkies, molded me and modeled to me what true friendship looks like, and we had the best time in the midst of it all.

Then there's Chloe: your soulmate, the one who speaks their mind, provides you whatever it is you're lacking on your own, tells you the truth (no matter how bluntly the words are spoken), and helps to give you meaning in your story. She also offers her blessing when it's in your best interest: for you to take the plunge on writing your story first because she's believed in it—and you—since day one.

I hope you have a Zach. Although it may not be readily apparent as to why they would be a key character, the reality is your first true love is essential since they instill hope inside you. You learn that even if love doesn't last between the two of you, love *does* exist. They were a part of your story to open you up to love, and they helped your heart expand in the process. You need your "Zach" to understand what you deserve . . . and what you *don't*. Although you might not end up right for each other, they are in the chapters of your life at the right time.

And you can't forget about Ella, the one who keeps things lighthearted, is always enjoyable to spend time with, and might even be the one who effortlessly matches you with your spouse (as she did), unintentionally locking themselves into your story for good. Friends like Ella are a constant in your life. They offer support, advice, and answers to your tough questions when you need to hear an honest answer.

The "Finding the Love of your Life" sermon gave me three points for the person I should marry, which confirmed to me why I was still single. Soon after I found the one who checked off all three prerequisites. I knew, even during the tough stuff, he was still likely my life partner.

Marrying Jude confirmed that spending my life with my best friend is possible; he pushes me to achieve my wildest dreams. Jude continues to say or text, "Good Morning, Beautiful," and he hasn't missed a morning since the week we met, no matter how many years into marriage we are or how many crazy kids keep us up the night before. When you find your match, you prioritize each other and work as a team.

Your Lucas is the one who shows up, puts in the effort, and doesn't make excuses. The sadness I still feel that he's no longer here is a telling reminder of how special he was to me and how someone can impact you so significantly, even years after they are gone. I hope you have someone who supports you, encourages you, and believes in you even before you believe in yourself.

Then there was the sermon "When God Says No" that gave my heart peace for the first time after losing one of my closest childhood friends. It reminds us that He is in control and has the ultimate perspective. Losing Lucas shifted my mindset and left me truly treasuring the relationships I have; it also instilled a grace and understanding within me for people with addiction or other issues that take hold of them.

What about that relationship with your built-in best friend? That best friend being *you*. The relationship you have with yourself is the longest one you will ever have. You choose how you talk to yourself and how you build yourself up daily (or break yourself down). You are the one who knows all those obstacles you've overcome and how much you've grown as a result. Take pride in your journey, set boundaries, and don't forget to love yourself.

In coherence with all these relationships, I allowed the Holy Spirit to take up space in my soul. He plays a big role in the essence of me.

First Thessalonians 5:23 talks about when He is a part of our life, that is when the three areas, spirit, body, and soul, are in balance. Proverbs 3:5–6 reminds us that "He will make your paths straight." When there were times I felt blinded while on my trail, it was me holding onto anxiety when I should have been leaning into His Word. And Psalm 91:1 reminds us that we have the choice to live in the "The shadow of the almighty" (also known as in the presence of God). No matter how dark our world may feel or seem, looking to God is looking to the light and enables us to feel peace.

As we travel along our individual paths toward this endless destiny of ourselves, we can try to avoid the storm clouds that inevitably come our way, or we can dance in the rainstorm. We have a choice to resist or to delicately choose how we react and respond to the curveballs life throws at us. After the storm clouds pass and the shadows decrease, the once-dark situation has the ability to display an even more beautiful scene than what was there before. This allows for a clearer perspective to shine through and an even more fulfilled person to appreciate the view.

It was those exact moments: the fog clearing and allowing me to observe Machu Picchu, gazing at the bright shining stars on the dock in Arizona while discussing burnt pizza, and having the dark cloud leave my mind after losing Lucas that allowed me to fully experience life. In the midst of uncertainty, there were those notable moments of clarity. It reiterated to me that although I had felt torn for years—where I should be living and what I should be doing with my life—I was slowly being pieced back together. It was up to me to allow it to happen and to take the small steps to foster the change within me and the growth I had been suppressing. Sometimes, it may take traveling a dark, overwhelming, or scary trail before we make it to the top of the mountain or enduring the confusing pile-of-goo stage before we transform into a delicate butterfly.

Take a moment to answer these questions:

- What metric for measuring true success or happiness am I using?
- Am I choosing to play it safe by living in security instead of discovering overwhelming freedom?
- Am I failing time and time again to fill the void inside by placing the right person, place, or thing to bring about the feeling of contentment?

If we choose to live in the complacency of comfort and shy away from venturing into the unknown, we may be solidifying our life to be perpetually unfulfilled, no matter how we try to rationalize it in our minds. If your purpose seems hazy, let me ask you: (1) What lights you up? and (2) What breaks your heart? This should help guide you to discovering your passions and what could point you in the right direction to fill the empty void inside.

Small steps in the right direction can affect how and what you think and have the potential to transform your life. Similar to the Butterfly Effect, it could create massive shifts in your final result or destination. Be brave enough to stray from what's easy or predictable and attempt your big and bold dreams. It doesn't matter where you're starting from, it just matters that you start.

Opalescent

I used to think life would provide me a black-and-white narrative. But I quickly encountered the gray areas and moments of complete blackout where I felt left in the dark. After some time, I shifted my course, my eyes, and my heart toward the light. I embraced my own shadow, defined my shining moments, held onto the sparkling memories, and I've learned how to accept the full colorful spectrum life gives to all of us. If you live a long and beautiful life, you will learn to love and appreciate all the colors life emits, even during the times or shades you don't like. Because altogether, it paints the portrait of your story. I've experienced the full array of light and dark times, but even during the darkest moments, there was always a glimmer of hope or opportunity that shone through.

One evening while putting my kids to bed, I reminded my eager daughter to "shh" as we were rocking her little brother to sleep. There was a round ceramic lamp on the side table next to the rocker that cast a glow throughout the entire room. The lamp, covered in cutouts of stars and moons, projects the galactic shapes on the walls and ceiling when it's switched on.

Falling asleep in my arms, my son's eyes blinked slowly until they stayed shut. My daughter stood right by his side.

Ready to tell her to hush or to give him space, I intently watched and waited for her next move. She gazed at his little face, then gave him a kiss on the forehead.

She started to caress his head and sing a song that I would often sing, Coldplay's song "Yellow."

She sang the words in her sweet toddler voice.

I felt a wave of peace. I've learned, just as she, her brother, and their little sister will too, that the stars shine through the dark clouds when they are supposed to, the fog clears to shift perspective for the unimaginable to appear, the shadows enhance the overall scene, and the caterpillar undergoes its gooey transformation to grow its wings to fly. The most unbelievable and amazing life can be lived when we embrace all it has to offer.

Trust your inner compass, as it's been inside you all along. Take note of your key characters or those other small glimmers or guiding lights steering your path. And never be afraid to expose your shadows to then shine your light. The world needs more of it.

Notes

Introduction

1. Nathan Chandler, "What Is the Butterfly Effect and How Do We Misunderstand It?" updated June 9, 2023, How Stuff Works, https://science.howstuffworks.com/math-concepts/butterfly-effect.htm.

Chapter 1: Perspective

1. Owen Jarus, "Machu Picchu: The Incan Estate 8,000 Feet High in the Andes," updated Aug. 3, 2023, Live Science, https://www.livescience.com/22869-machu-picchu.html.

Chapter 17: Chrysalis

1. Elizabeth Scott, "What Is a Highly Sensitive Person (HSP)? updated June 13, 2023, Very Well Mind, https://www.verywellmind.com/highly-sensitive-persons-traits-that-create-more-stress-4126393.

Chapter 18: Butterfly

1. Vivian Bricker, "What is the Dark Night of the Soul," updated March 8, 2023, Christianity, https://www.christianity.com/wiki/christian-life/what-is-the-dark-night-of-the-soul.html.
2. Casey Leins, "Millions of Butterflies Migrate across California," March 14, 2019, *US News & World Report*, https://www.usnews.com/news/best-states/articles/2019-03-14/millions-of-butterflies-migrate-across-california.

www.ingramcontent.com/pod-product-compliance
Lightning Source LLC
LaVergne TN
LVHW100525110826
845146LV00002B/777